DOG BOOK

Durham NC   DEC 18 2003

Karen,
DAVID, Josephine
& Jonas —
May the perfect
dog finds you!

Emily Eve Weinstein

DOG BOOK

Beau Soleil
publishing

Library of Congress Catalog Card Number: 2003114015

ISBN: 0-9746279-0-9 Cloth
        0-9746279-1-7 Trade Paper

First Edition, First Printing

Printed in South Korea

Design: Mia Blume

Editorial Coordination:
John Patrick Grace
Grace Associates, LLC
945 4th Avenue Suite 200A
Huntington, West Virginia 25701

Artist Photograph: David Jessee
Digital Image Color Correction:
Ken Crossen

Beau Soleil Publishing
P.O. Box 2395
Huntington, West Virginia 25724

table of contents

acknowledgements

A special thanks to the following who
greatly supported this project:

Amanda Ballard
Mia Blume
Anne Bogerd
Jennifer Collins
Ken Crossen
Patrick Grace
David Jessee
Anne McKenna
Jeff Sells
Linda Tilley
Dietrich von Haugwitz
Debby Weinstein
Norman Weinstein
and all the dogs and their people.

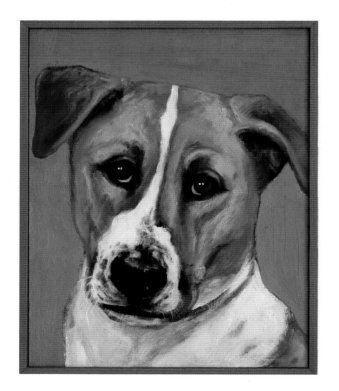

introduction

Dog Book is a natural step after Cat Book, although the art work is very different. With this latest project I'm taking a large series of photos and then composing the image by doing several pencil sketches. Then I transpose my ideas to board. When the painting nears completion, the canine subject visits my studio and I do the final touch-up live, which takes me 45 minutes to four hours. Some dogs prove to be terrible models, and In those instances I do very little more to the painting. Others sit very well for those final improvements. With Rachel, a Doberman, I was able to re-do her entire portrait, every hair! With chow-corgy mix Monkey, forget it! She is in your face with "the tongue." Treats, of course, help greatly.

For this project I went to the local shelter and adopted the quintessential mutt, a dog that encompasses all breeds. She is very athletic, and her personality is loving, protective, adventurous, friendly, perceptive. Why ever did I wait so long to adopt another dog? I truly forgot how much joy, love and exercise a dog companion brings into one's life. Going away has not been a problem. She happily stays with friends that have dogs and a fenced yard. The positives far outweigh any negatives.

Dogs inspire loyalty, play and adventure, but their uncanny ability to sense things make them invaluable. Not long ago, less than two years old, China gets me out of bed at 12:30 a.m. by pacing and whining. Once out, she pulls me determinedly in the opposite direction from the way we normally go. There before us is our neighbor lying prone. The ambulance arrives quickly; she is now making a good recovery from a stroke. China often astounds me.

My subjects are not simply all the dogs and people I knew before or were led to. A chapter is devoted to the rescue K-9s of 9/11. Then, in order to raise funds for Animal Haven in Queens, New York, another chapter in the book is being auctioned off,

Jenna and Abby   9" x 4.5"   Graphite on paper

with the winning bidder's dog to be included. Most recently I met the incredible Ginny, the dog that rescues cats. Thus, to understate it, creating this book has been a huge adventure, one I hope you'll share with me from the beginning to the end. Happy trails!

Choreographing the Leashes
15" x 12"
Graphite on paper

In Memory of Eva von Haugwitz

Dedicated to animal activists everywhere

Sumi on the Go! | The studio door is stuck open because of a fallen ladder. A small dog works her way around the obstacles and settles down on the cement floor with a sigh of exhaustion. The cats look at her with only mild interest. We have never seen her before. My new neighbor Eileen stops by. "Oh, Sumi, you found cats to hang out with?" Sumi stretches, yawns loudly and gets up to join her human.

They have just come in from Chicago, a twelve–hour road trip. I ask how the trip went. Sumi loved every second of it, pehaps the highlight of her fourteen years: wind whistling through her ears, sitting on Mom's lap for hours, flashing images, new friends, roadside treats and roadside smells. Travel and adapting to new surroundings is what Sumi is all about.

As just a wee tyke at the Marina Del Rey shelter, Sumi is enroute to the front door with the rest of her litter mates. She escapes and runs right into the arms of a man called Jerry. Jerry picks her up, instantly knowing that his quest for a big sturdy walking dog is over. He has fallen in love with a puppy that will never grow higher than his calf.

The long hikes Jerry had anticipated are instead long bike rides. They are known all over town, and Sumi is greatly admired in her basket. Sumi takes to boating, running around the deck, basking in the sun with a slight spray misting her face as she catches all the wonderful smells of the ocean and occasionally barks her commands. Frequently they fly to Michigan to visit Jerry's family, friends and his ex-wife, Eileen. Sumi stays with Eileen, who loves her almost as much as Jerry does.

When Jerry is diagnosed with lung cancer, Eileen agrees Sumi should be with her. Before moving to Michigan perma-

Sumi   18"x14"   Oil on board

nently, Sumi provides support to Jerry in his last days. Eileen, realizing the orphaned dog has lived a life of action, takes her everywhere; when she can't, Sumi goes to Kathy's Dog Camp, where she frolics along a pond with a Yorky named Suzy. They chase squirrels and play all day. Here at Solterra she walks into new places and makes them all hers.

China's World | It has been two and a half years since Daisy Mae passed over to the other side. I'm beginning *Dog Book*, thinking about finding an ambassador to this project, when Susan Teer tells me the current dismal statistics regarding overpopulation. Okay, it is time to make a commitment.

Enroute to the shelter I make mental notes about the dog I'm about to adopt: a ready–made that won't jump up, walks well on a leash and is house-broken, someone I can pick up

Maybe Tomorrow   9˝ x 7˝   Oil on board

and put in the tub, but is big enough to intimidate an assailant, is three years or older and sturdy enough for a ten-mile hike. With this list vaguely in mind, I walk down the interior corridor and then the exterior corridor, reviewing close to 100 dogs. I see a beautiful liver-colored pit bull, three blue-eyed huskies, a white German shepherd, and several black Labs. On my second walk around, a dog I had completely overlooked walks to the front of her cage. Our eyes lock in instant contact.

In the visiting room she shakes all over—the cats will be safe, as she can be intimidated. Outside she walks without pulling the lead, does her business, and in the sunshine reveals herself as the strong, healthy girl she is. I take a deep breath and pay the adoption fee in full. She can't go home with me for five days as she arrived as a stray only two days ago. The dog who by now I have named Amy Ray, watches as I leave.

From my studio I phone Sonja, the woman that turned the stray in. "That dog is not a stray. I lied. I've had China since she was a puppy. I love her, but with four kids to support and her needing to be spayed, someone had to go." Whoa! How old is she? "Not quite eight months. Born March 10th, 2001. "Yikes! She is getting bigger? "Her brother Japan is huge. We kept him, as he doesn't have to be spayed." Neutered? "Yes, but it can wait until I have funds. It just didn't make sense risking puppies."

Friends were stunned by China's story. How could somebody relinquish her baby dog to a shelter? In her situation Sonja did the best she could. China was never abused, never went hungry, as her weight demonstrates, or had unwanted puppies, was not given to an inadequate home or abandoned on the highway or dropped off in the woods. Sonja strongly believed she would be recognized for the perfect dog she is and be given a perfect home. She prayed for this, and then she received my phone call. Sonja called the shelter so China could go to her new home the next day.

Somehow at my house, she looks much larger. Within two days the cats are rubbing up against her. Roma, the black cat, adopts her, as he did Daisy Mae before her. He snuggles beside her in the new doggy bed, takes the morning and evening walk with her, tripping through her legs.

Christmas/Chanukah arrives. China has only been with me a month, so I stay in town. Feeling left out and alone, with China I go to K-Mart and buy a gift for each member of her first family. I wrap the gifts in the parking lot and then we drive straight to their house. Everyone is delighted to see China, including enormous brother Japan. Now the holiday feels complete.

Detail of China from Water Dogs

China's Friends | Every day China acquires a little more socialization. Behind us lives Cleatus, a gentle English Labrador whom she bounces about with. Down the trail live

Jenna & Abby
9"x4.5" Pencil

Isabelle, a springer spaniel, and Zanna, a blond Lab. Water, of any quality, magnetically attracts them. Not China, but she is fast learning from them. Zanna & China are tight. When Zanna makes a break from her home, she bee-lines the 400 yards straight to China, hitting the front door with her paw and barking a few choice words: "Come out and play with me!" I then get a call from her person. "Zanna there?" Yeah. "I'll be over in an hour." Meanwhile the girls play in the big field, where Zanna leads China into mud every time.

Sierra, a flat-coated collie, lives past Zanna and Isabelle. When we go for walks, someone will ask, "Are they from the same litter? Same breed?" And then adds, "Funny, there is something different between your twin dogs." Yeah, I'll say! Shape, fur, face, age, weight, ears, temperament, and cost! Oh well, what the two do share is near–identical coloring and markings. By being dominant, China has unwit-tingly taught Sierra how to stand her ground. China allows Sierra to knock her down upon occasion, which for a chow-pit-Akita-hound–mix is good–natured. Thankfully, Sierra's young human, Sabrina, gets out of the way when the two beasts flip each other around.

Most of the canine residents in the hood are China's friends, but some elude her. One household has a large shepherd that is nervous around other dogs. We avoid him. Daphne is a good–hearted lab that greets China with hugs and kisses, but with her person they are always off and run-ning. In two years she has played with Daphne only twice.

Water Dogs   22" x 18"   Oil on board

New neighbors are moving in with extremely playful dogs, Jenna and Abby. With them and others on our team, we are forming a dog park: 100' x 100' of fencing, a picnic table in shade, and an orchard of fruit trees above.

Sierra and China   21" x 16"   Oil on board

Separated at Birth
8" x 7"   Graphite on paper

Reversal of Fortune |

Magic

Marcello of Animal Haven in Flushing, New York, has to make some tough decisions. He is approached by a man with a dog. "You must take this dog. I'm about to be homeless and I know you won't kill him." True, Animal Haven is a no-kill shelter, but they are working at maximum capacity. "I'm sorry, very sorry for your predicament, but no, we can't take him."

Next morning the wiry, scared dog is found tied to the Haven's gate, the man nowhere in sight. Where there is no room, some is made, and the mixed breed is dubbed Surrender. Surrender is cleaned up and included in the next booth set-up in Central Park, where he is noticed by a family. Melissa senses this is a gentle dog, perfect for her two boys and daughter. Her husband James agrees. The kids are unanimous.

During the interview Marcello discovers that James is a lawyer, and even more important, willing to work pro bono on behalf of animals. Animal Haven thus acquires a strong legal connection, and Surrender is renamed Magic. Quite a coup!

At home Magic makes some easy adjustments, others not so easy. The elderly dachshund poses no competition, but many things scare him. While he is trying to form new bonds with this enthusiastic family, he still wonders where his original person is. Magic's new home overlooks Central Park East, where he goes for walks. Weekends he is being introduced to new and wonderful sights and smells at the country place, where he runs free along the beach. Still, there is a deep sadness that will remain with him a long time.

A couple of years later the family stops by the Haven's adoptathon booth at the Times Square Visitor's Center and selects another mix-breed dog. Ally is a doofy large puppy with a good nature. No bad memories in her short life. Wrong. The Center for Animal Care and Control found her in an alley with a long gash down her neck. They get her stitched up and contact Animal Haven to find her a good home. She now has one with her five humans and companion, Magic, whom she works hard to annoy.

Magic is highly tolerant of the young Ally, but he keeps all other dogs away from his family. He might be thinking, "Things are just fine as they are. Let's keep them that way."

Central Park

Ally

Magic & Ally
in Central Park
24"x20"
Oil on board

Miss Lucy and Ursula

| June 8th, with my folks and good friend Mandy, we troop out to Queens for the Animal Haven Auction at the Veterans of Foreign Affairs building. I'm autographing *Cat Book* as part of this fund raiser, and also a chapter in *Dog Book* is being auctioned off. Anne McKenna is high bidder, and so her fourteen–year–old canine companions, Lucy and Ursula, have won a place in infamy.

I stay in Manhattan when in New York, Anne McKenna being way the heck out in Middle Village. Yep, that is right smack next to Middle Earth. Well, no, not really, but with the twists and turns Middle Earth seems not very far off. So she very generously comes into the city to pick me up.

She lives with Lucy and Ursula on a quiet corner. On her front stoop are dishes for local strays she feeds and occasionally traps to neuter and release. Her grandfather built three duplexes all right here, circa 1930. Ms. McKenna has always lived in one of them.

Upstairs she houses three cat colonies of unadoptable cats, and downstairs there are seven cats that get along well with the shepherd–greyhound Lucy and Ursula the chow. Miss Lucy keeps the cats in line. This climbing up on cupboards and scratching of furniture she keeps to a minimum. With polydactyl Polly there is a tight bond, much hugging and kissing, a regular love fest between hound and multi–toed cat. Lucy does not like my intrusion into her home, but allows me to scratch her behind the

Ursula

ears. Ursula is more adaptable, but follows Lu's lead when it comes to barking. These old girls have their comfortable routines.

Ursula hardly notices she lives with cats. With Lucy she argues, making noises between growling and yawning. She appears glad I'm here and smiles, revealing her black–purplish tongue. Fourteen years ago, along with all the other chows from a backyard breeder, she is dropped off at Animal Haven. The breeder, realizing his profit is inadequate, threatens to abandon all of them unless The Haven takes the lot! So a fluffy young chow goes home with Ms. McKenna. Hers is one of the overflow households of the no–kill shelter.

A squatter that collects animals contacts The Haven regarding a young dog she feels needs medical care. Anne takes young Lucy to Dr. Tobias, who discovers a broken leg and pelvis. After the delicate surgery the dog can neither be returned to the squatter nor The Haven; home she goes with Anne. Fourteen years later she still sports a pin in one leg. Dr. Tobias has retired, but his assistant went back to school to get her veterinarian license and is now Dr. Vollel, having bought her boss's practice. In any case, these dogs and thirty–plus cats have had very consistent lives, from vets to home.

Lucy

I ask Anne McKenna how she became involved with Animal Haven. "Back in 1974 I volunteered only on Saturdays, cleaning cat cages. When I retired from teaching high school English, I was able to devote more time. Particularly when they found out I could edit the newsletter." How involved are you now? "Oh, I'm the board president."

Now I'm very glad she is high bidder, as her dependable kindness and generosity of spirit are recorded here forever.

Ursule and Lucy   23˝ x 20˝   Oil on board

Divine Intervention | In the small town of Kennebunkport, Maine, Pat Marsters enters the vet's office with Tuesday, a blue-cream tortie. Nothing can be done for the sweet 18-year-old cat. Whether the end is today, tomorrow or the day after, Pat is preparing for the inevitable. In the reception room is a forlorn-looking cocker. Pat bends down, asking, "And who do we have here?" The dog looks up with his sad gaze. Barkley is twelve and his person has just died; no provisions made. He has been dropped off to be neutered. In this small town the animal shelter rules are unbending: all animals must be altered, no exceptions. So here's Barkley, a senior canine, one testicle undescended, a history of seizures, deemed unadoptable, about to undergo a normally simple procedure that could kill him.

Realizing Barkley's precarious situation, Pat fills out an application to adopt him on the spot. Heading to work and throughout the day, she worries about him. Will he survive?... He does. Her application is approved; she has no competition.

When the old dog recovers from the operation, he sniffs around his new home and likes it. Pat's 100+ year old Cape Cod is homey, with a wood stove in the kitchen, low wood ceilings, throw rugs covering the floor for those cold Maine mornings. New home and new name.... Pat explains to Barkley that her childhood dog was Bugsy. Could they maybe adjust his name to be Mr. Bugsy Barkley? Just as he took to his new home, he takes to his new name. Fergus the cat, however, doesn't view the meeting of Bugsy and his person as divine intervention. To the tabby this is a terrible mistake. To change his mind, Bugsy stops chasing him and becomes respectful and calm as the desires of the cat dictate.

With the chickens, Pat discovers the dog's need for order. Bugsy herds the flock, moving them into a tighter clutch. He

Bugsy Barkley Jones

Bugsy Barkley Jones   18" x 23"   Oil on board

quickly becomes a watch dog over his chickens as his protective bark keeps away fox and raccoon. He loves other birds, too, especially ducks and their poop! Across the street is a duck pond set in a large meadow filled with aromatic droppings. Bugsy can just roll and roll and roll all day in that stuff. Fortunately he also enjoys baths. He loves being fussed over. The ocean, too, often helps eliminate his eagerly collected scents. No matter how frigid the temperature, Bugsy goes straight into the water.

Pat works as the recreational therapist at the Renaissance Nursing Home. When Bugsy is healed, she takes him along. He is a natural therapy dog, intuitively knowing how to relate to everyone. For those unresponsive he rests his head on their knee. He sits next to wheelchairs to be stroked and jumps up when more gregarious attention is required. During bowling he strolls around the rolling balls, cracking everyone up. In exercise class he wiggles about the floor, music class he joins in. Music excites him because it transports him back to when he was

unaltered. Bugsy becomes the class Casanova, humpimg the wheel chairs of the elderly women. When his person, Pat, dances with a male resident, he interrupts. Pat then picks up his two front paws and dances with him instead. This he prefers. Soon after the cocker's arrival at the nursing home residents that rarely participated now do. They want to see Bugsy, have his head in their laps, pet his fleecy soft fur, and perhaps even experience his odd form of dancing. From the

beginning Pat's boss is delighted with the dog's influence. Bugsy has turned around many near catatonics.

On Wednesdays other therapy dogs visit the nursing home, and Bugsy has a day off. Enroute to her job, Pat drops him off at her good friend Connie's house. Connie is teaching herself how to play piano. In the beginning Bugsy noticeably does not like her playing, but in time his music appreciation develops and he settles at her feet. When it gets close to leaving time, he picks up all his toys and drops them into the laundry basket. At home with Pat he prefers to have his toys all over the place. About the approximate time Pat leaves work, Bugsy starts pacing. When she arrives and before they go, he places his paws on Connie's lap and gazes into her eyes. "Thank you for having me over." Bugsy is the perfect gentleman visitor.

From the moment Pat adopts him till just a week before his passing, Mr. Bugsy Barkley has brought three years of companionship, humor, understanding, joy, and affection to hundreds of seniors. The nursing home dedicates a mass to Bugsy and priest that officiates at his funeral tells how his dog phobia has disappeared by his knowing Bugsy and his great heart. Flowers fill Pat's home, the shelves are covered with sympathy cards for the old dog that was almost anonymously euthanized three years earlier.

Princess Camille | Anne calls. "It's Camille's birthday this Saturday, and my neighbor said I could invite you." You see, Camille is a most unusual English spaniel–mix. She was originally adopted by her humans, Kay and Dean, from the Houston SPCA. She hates water, and fetching holds absolutely no interest.

It is June 14th, Flag Day, and the closest approximation of when she would have been born fifteen years ago. The birthday girl is friendly towards the two–legged animals and for this occasion is even being tolerant towards the four-legged kind. There are nine other canines: Ralph the Scottish deerhound; Haley, a Doberman pinscher; Amigo, a chocolate Lab; BJ, an

Camille and George   21" x 25"   Oil on board

apricot poodle; and several Lhasa apsos. Someone has also shown up with a very personable Boston terrier.

The table is stacked high with dog gifts, and a scrumptious cake has been flown in from Three Dog Bakery. It is their peanut butter carob with vanilla icing. Some of the taller dogs are trying to get a bite before serving time.

Camille

A year later I'm invited back for Camille's 16th birthday, but unfortunately I'm out of town. Kay recounts that it has been an excellent decade and a half with this unlikely spaniel. One Sunday her husband Dean is out walking with Zack, their first adopted dog. Zack sees a friend across the street and runs to greet him. Instantly he is struck and killed. His sudden departure is unbearable. The thought of coming home that Monday and not seeing Zack's nose poking through the venetian blinds, Zack waiting for her, is nothing Kay can stand. Monday morning she is at the shelter as the doors are unlocked. And fifteen-week-old Camille enters her life.

During her first month Camille keeps her tail tucked between her legs. Loud noises, fast movements, all scare her. Kay and Dean look forward to when Camille will blossom into the water dog she is meant to be. Well, that never happens, but she will chase after a thrown rock or golf ball. It just never occurs to her to return it. She loves snow, but ungroomed trails are a nuisance. She is very particular about her feet. She prefers city sidewalks to a path with sticks and leaves. In every way Camille is very sensitive to her physical world. Kay grooms her as she goes into a long sequence of low yips, mounting into an entire sonata of sounds and whines, ending like a completed composition. Very strange.

Camille has been cancer-free for three years. She is on amitriptyline for her obsessive/compulsive disorder. Unfortunately the drug does not help with her separation anxiety, but now Kay works at home. Most recently our mutual friend Anne had a handsome pastel-marmalade cat show up. She names him George. Kay and Dean are not interested in giving him a home, so Anne places an ad. (Newspapers will run free ads for lost or found animals, but it is best not to use the word "free" in the text.) Subsequently George finds a home across town. A couple weeks later George reappears. K & D reconsider.

This morning George brings his new family a freshly killed squirrel. Camille is delighted to smell one of these animals close up. In her entire life she has never caught one herself. George brings an added dimension to her life, and the occasional nuzzle.

It's drizzling out. George is stretched out on the couch, his feet touching Camille. I suggest we go outside. We do momentarily. George goes off in search of more "gifts" while Camille turns back to the house..."too cold, too wet, too unpleasant." The old girl has a few solid birthdays left. Her folks take very good care of her, and it seems the orange fellow George will play a part in that effort, too.

George

Daisy Mae | Parking in back of the food co-op, I see a few dogs waiting outside for their people. As I approach, this wiry, wild-haired blond one is wiggling on the ground towards me, lifting her upper lip intermittently in a toothy grin. Her eyes are a pale golden hue with flecks of olive green, her nose a pale liver color with freckles. This is the oddest looking and behaving canine I have ever seen.

In the co-op I ask, "Who is the weird, slithering, grinning dog?" Erin Sweeney responds, "That's Daisy Mae. She approached you? Normally she's scared of everyone. A couple moved out and left her and other animals behind about a year ago. It took me six months before I could touch her. The dog catcher came out many times, but she's too smart. She hid well. She still has a way to go, but we have five rescues at home. Are you interested in her?" I left, saying I'd think about it. Outside she now stands up and wiggles all over at me, her head making these expressive twists. She is almost tap-dancing, doing her weird little grin. She knows something before I do.

The next day I phone Erin. Daisy Mae seems to think we belong together. Erin tells me to go by her place off Buchanan Boulevard, I'll find Daisy Mae there. Well, there she is, the blond, freckle-nosed terrier sitting on the front stoop. Without hesitation she bounces off and onto the passenger's seat of my truck like an old habit.

At the house the cats understand she is harmless as she lopes around her new yard. With her leash attached, we go for our first walk on Driver Street where I live. As a couple approaches us, Daisy Mae lunges desperately in all directions to avoid them. She repeats her terrified "Don't beat me!" behavior twice more before we get to the corner.

That night I'm invited to an intimate little potluck. The hostess Kara says, "Oh, please, bring Daisy Mae so we can meet her!" I'm not sure I should, remembering the walk, but I do. Of course, the dog spends the evening shaking under a couch. What have I adopted? I phone Erin Sweeney the following morning at the co-op: "What happened to this dog?" "She

Daisy Mae   12" x 10"   Oil on board

was running around fending for herself, eating out of garbage cans. Kids chased her on bikes, and at least one car hit her. She had a litter, but they were either born dead or killed. The pound came out many times to get her, but she was too wily for them and she was never caught. It took me six months to gain this dog's trust. It's a miracle she's alive. She's doing great, considering all." Oh boy, I'm thinking, this is great?

I get a position as a visiting artist in the middle of North Carolina, so I move to the quaint country town of Troy with cats Opal and Zia and severely neurotic Daisy Mae. In my newfound position I am to demonstrate various modes of art, create several murals at the community college, and meet with every class in the public school system at least once. Living with an

Daisy Mae   12" x 10"   Oil on board

abused animal, I'm feeling that there is nothing more important than spreading the word of animal welfare all wrapped up in a package of animal art! So, equipped with slide presentation, art supplies and trembling dog, we enter our first school. The students are loud but become subdued and curious when they see Daisy Mae. I explain we need complete silence because of what she has been through. Then I ask, "Is there someone that would like to be her guardian? Who is going to sit up here and protect her?" Everyone wants to, with both hands up and loud pleas, "Oh, me, me, me, please choose me...." The chosen student claims a place next to the terrier, looking very smug. The protective arm goes around Daisy and the slide show begins. I talk about water colors versus pastel, overpopulation, altering pets, rendering a likeness, grooming, painting fur and other textures, animal nutrition and exercise. When the lights come on, Daisy Mae has melted into the child's lap and is looking very comfortable.

On brown paper I do a portrait of Daisy Mae while every student is edging closer to pet her wiry fur. When the class ends I remind all within earshot to make sure all their pets are altered, exercised, well nourished, and adored because they are just as special as Daisy Mae. After a month of repeating "Animal Art," the dog becomes kid-proof, walking calmly in crowds, asking for attention from everyone, and getting it. Thunder and lightning still terrify her and always will.

Feeling confident and adventurous, Daisy Mae learns how to push open doors and nudge out of windows. One day I get a call from the sleepy town of Troy: "Daisy Mae is here visiting." Evidently she has taken herself on a walk several blocks away and found a nice couple to accompany. They all enter a house and are invited to sit down. Daisy Mae happily flops on the couch beside them. The hostess comments on their unusual dog. "Huh? You mean she doesn't live here? She isn't ours! She isn't yours?" Fortunately they phone the number on her tag and I drive over. She doesn't want to go. Dinner is just being served and she has already eaten the cat's food. We are invited to stay. I apologize for Ms. Terrier Boldness and we leave. I now have a whole set of new problems.

At my next residency we get to live at the coast. Daisy has never experienced the ocean. At first timid, within days it is all hers. She dances straight into the waves, running along the shore grinning. Her wiry blond coat, completely curled, acts like a golden sun-catcher. She loves exploring sand castles, digging the moat around them deeper but never disturbing the structure.

She still accompanies me to schools and my office. Through the local arts council I organize an exhibition called Animals in Art, with 40 percent of sales going to the local animal welfare group. We have over 200 participants. During classes on animal art I touch on the theme of compassion and welfare, but my model is no longer convincing as she tap-dances, grinning, shaking her head left and then right, demanding attention from all that meet her.

Daisy Mae at Holden Beach   5.5" x 7.5"   Lineoleum print

Griffin Grape | My friend Nathan and I have a few things in common. The most obvious is looking at me right now, Griffin, a most handsome terrier–mix. For eleven years I lived with a dog, Daisy Mae, who looked like a relative of Griffin's AND she was rescued from the same neighborhood fifteen years earlier. They both spend a full year learning to be less fearful. Fortunately Griffin is very young when Durham Animal Control finds him walking along Buchanan Boulevard with his mother and sister. Griffin's mother, reportedly too sick for what the shelter can do for her, is euthanized. The sister is adopted by a graduate student, a very attractive one, Nathan adds. Griffin was already adopted but is soon returned "for something terrible he'd done." Back with the APS, they bathe him and he goes ballistic. Now they are debating whether they can responsibly place him at all. In walks Nathan, out walks Griffin with him.

Nat is a writer, so like me he can't help but investigate Griff's background. He calls the grad student that adopted his sister. The dogs are reunited in Duke Gardens, romping, playing,

Griffin and Nathan   5.5" x 8"   Graphite on paper

Griffin

having a marvelous time. This is Griffin's final memory of his sister, for soon after, attractive graduate with dog moves away. Nathan is more disappointed than Griffin.

At their home, filled with retro collections and antiques, Griffin hospitably gives me a tour. His backyard is about a hundred feet square, with a stream running through it. Nat fenced it to further assist G's need for security, but the dog prefers being inside or beside his human. He keeps watch on everything Nat does. In bed he sleeps closer to the door in case

he has to attack an intruder. When Nat goes to work he becomes a diligent watch dog from upstairs on his bed. Griffin never takes his toys out of the house. He drops them at the door before continuing outside. N believes this is a sign of his lingering fear of abandonment.

"Griffin likes you." I'm not flattered, and I explain that he seems like the kind of guy that shows everyone his belly and kisses one and all. "Not true. He growls when my girlfriend goes to hug him, and he is not any more hospitable to my parents." How's that? "My parents bought a bichon frise. When my brother asked why didn't they look for a Griffin, they replied he's not a purebred. And then they got to witness how he helps me with the dishes. Griff gets to rinse them off, and...well...they haven't eaten at my house since." Pretty much sealed the deal. And that is okay. Nat's folks now stay elsewhere when in town, as "the mutt" has not been the sweet hospitable kinda guy that I've met. Griffin poses beautifully for me as if he understands the objective.

Another thing Nathan and I have in common is that as long as this world has strays, we will not be supporting breeders.

Griffin Grape   20" x   20"   Oil on board

Milly's Angel | Every day I get emails about a litter needing to be placed, cats needing foster care, dogs needing transportation to a no-kill facility. In one such email, I open the photo and there is this image of a slack-jawed, near-toothless, crystal-blue-eyed-mix with a woman holding her. The email goes on to state that the dog dubbed Milly has lived at Kerr Lake for years, producing many puppies. Currently, another litter is at large, but completely feral, and when caught, where to put them? Am I interested in fostering Milly? Unfortunately, facing a fast-approaching book deadline, I can't, but I am anxious to follow her story.

Next email: "It seems Milly is quite old, has mammary tumors, heartworms, and can't receive treatment for any of it due to her fragile condition. Who wants to foster until a permanent home is found for her remaining time?" Many pitiful stories come through, but this one is right up there. What angel might come through for this most unlikely adoptee? Well, about the same time I get this email, so does Kim Hinton, at work an hour away.

At the State Bureau of Investigation east of Raleigh, Milly's blue-eyed, almost-toothless image appears on Kim's monitor. An intern walks by and comments, "That is the ugliest dog I've ever seen." Kim feels hurt for the dog and wonders if everyone will dismiss Milly so curtly. That does it! She spins back an email saying she will adopt Milly. I, too, have emailed: "Whatever angel adopts this dog is definitely included in *Dog Book*!"

I trek out to meet Milly in the country suburbs and am greeted by Border collie–mix Brutus. Milly is subdued but friendly, rising from her bed in the living room. She is recognizable from the miserable photo I was sent, but her coat looks good and she's very much at home. Kim adds, "Milly didn't want to explore, she wanted simply to be able to relax and

Detail from Milly at Home

sleep. At night she gets anxious, like she needs to go collect food or maybe find her puppies. Last night for the first time she was no longer anxious."

Milly was discovered by Vicky of Best Friends Pet Adoption after attending her new church near her weekend home on Kerr Lake. The scraggly dog greets the congregation, going from person to person, seeking food and affection. Her blood-engorged ticks are obvious, her face welted up from their bites. Despite the discomfort she must be in, she is friendly to all. Vicky can't take her home because she has a haphazard house full of cats, being a foster home for Best Friends. She is told the dog lives in what seems an abandoned shanty. Church members have been feeding her for years. Many litters of puppies have come and gone. As soon as Vicky can reach a phone, she calls Best Friends' founder, Susan Walker. There are no vacancies at Susan's house either, but she instructs Vicky to take photos of the sweet dog. Armed with camera, Vicki is surprised by a territorial derelict squatter in the rundown shack. Vicky begins stalking the place, driving by slowly to get a glimpse of the dog. This goes on for a couple of weekends. Finally the stray shows up, the scary vagrant is gone, and Vicky snaps Milly's image, capturing her two remaining teeth. Three older puppies are spotted. The email goes out; this is when Kim Hinton steps forward.

In answer to my question about how she got involved in animal rescue, Kim responds, "Candi, a dachshund, opened my heart to dogs. She was the love of my life. She lost a leg to cancer, but got around just fine on three." Rudy, Kim's husband, adds, "And then we lost the two Labs. They dug out from under the fence. Something must have attracted them in the woods. We found Samantha by the bridge, struck dead. Sam was buried by a local farmer, thinking it was his dog, but then his Lab came home. Our fence is now chain-link and electric. The dogs do not go near it." And indeed, the yard being huge, they don't need to. Outside I meet sturdy Mic, found by Rudy at work. "He looks like a junkyard dog, but he simply loves to

Milly at Home   14" x 24"   Oil on wood

play." Mic is a bouncy, chocolatey chow–pit–Lab–mix with a huge smile. With him is the black Lab foundling, Molly, who easily keeps up with him. Unless Milly does a complete turn-around, she will never even meet these large active dogs. "Oh, and what is the enclosure for?" There is a 20 x 40 chain–link pen inside the fenced area. "This Rudy installed," explains Kim, "in case Milly preferred to be outdoors, but she doesn't, so we'll be using it for dogs that turn up in the future."

Rudy heads out the door with Brutus for a car ride. When they return, we walk across the street for Brutus to visit his girlfriend, a Lab–mix. A car pulls in next door to Kim and Rudy's. Brutus runs over, greeting the man enthusiastically as he gets out of his truck. "Our next–door neighbor was his original home, but then Brutus needed treatment for heartworm. We shared the expense with other neighbors across the street next door to Brutus's girlfriend. During the day the original owner tells them about his beach trip and how he returned early because he missed the dog too much. I'm amazed at how this brilliant dog has such a grip on four households.

We bring Ms. blue-eyed Milly outside. She stands still. Being leashed is new to her. She walks about a little, very lit-tle. She wants to return inside. I ask if she's housebroken. Kim responds, "Better than that, no accidents inside and she relieves herself every other day. When she gets healthier, more secure, we are going to investigate what can be done to optimize her life." If she is able to go through heartworm treatment, she will be the fourth that Kim and Rudy have financed through this ordeal. I leave, feeling our email net-work is most remarkable. It works as long as good folks such as these step forward to rescue and care for such as Milly.

Brutus   11" x 9"   Graphite on paper

Sheila of Firehouse III

As my canine companion Daisy Mae and I pass the fire station, a Chihuahua–mix follows along with a sideways growl. A fireman starting up the station's barbecue grill explains, "You're not in uniform, you're not one of her people." So taking the challenge, I stop to convince her I'm okay. Sheila, also known as Wonder Dog, SheHe and Beana, is easily convinced and climbs partially into my lap. Daisy Mae she doesn't warm towards. She doesn't care for other dogs usurping any attention that belongs to her.

Firefighter Glen Elliott (Catfish) recalls sitting in the TV room eating a tuna fish sandwich and hearing the clicking of nails across the linoleum floor. "I look down and there is Sheila with that sparkle in her eye. This is the beginning of a long relationship." Soon after, Catfish takes his new friend for a ride in the fire truck. She sits on his lap, paws on the steering wheel. Sometimes she sits up higher on the part of the truck actually known as the "dog bed." From here Sheila gets a better view. When sirens sound she is ready to ride! "She has clocked thousands of miles with me, and she is known all over town."

Some people from Marietta, Georgia, walk up the street to reclaim their little dog. Not an hour later, Sheila is back. The grill is being fired up and she is first in line. I ask Catfish's son, firefighter Todd Elliott, about her eating habits, "She gets fed dog food, but snacks with whoever, and oh, she does love a cookout!" This I have witnessed as, driving by, I spot Sheila at the grill, surrounded by several hunky men. This is hard to miss.

Her original family make several attempts to bring her back "home," but then one day they come by and see her lower midriff is bandaged; she has just been spayed. Not only could they not compete with the fire-station food and outings,

Sheila of Fire House III   7" x 6"   Oil on board

they also would never have gotten her to a vet. Officer Buddy Christian makes sure she is well checked out and gets the standard shots. Soon, the people from Marietta, Georgia, move. It is doubtful Sheila noticed.

The neighborhood is rough. The alarm blasts for fires and other emergencies, but nothing protects cars from break-ins. That is, until Sheila arrives. She is protective of her firehouse, all within and their property. Would-be break-ins are inter-

Sheila with Catfish   5" x 4.5"
Graphite on paper

rupted by her barking. The crew learns the urgency by her tone. By averting many potential thefts, she makes even those most skeptical of her role more accepting.

When her primary people come on duty, Sheila is elated, showering them with ample enthusiasm. She sleeps on any of the beds, cuddling with whomever she shares a mutual affection. Most frequently she sacks out next to Buddy, Catfish, or Officer Elizabeth Parden, but then her snoring can be so loud that her companion of the moment places her outside the door. Besides a solid sleeping regimen and excellent diet, the dog gets her exercise. This is quite a sight: as many as seven men in shorts jogging around the block with fifteen pound Sheila taking up the rear. But then she gets wise. Halfway down the block she turns around and runs to the corner waiting. The men return breathing harder, having done the complete circle. They are greeted joyfully by Sheila, who is not at all out of breath!

The dog is not only a hit with the fire department, but also at schools during the annual fire-drill demonstrations. She is dressed in her little red sweater with her official patch sewn on back. The students get to look in the fire truck and see firefighter Buddy, who moves aside and they meet firetruck driver Catfish; he then moves aside and there between them is Wonder Dog Sheila, also in uniform. Of course, her appearance is the highlight of the event as all the children vie to pet her.

Sheila is spotted down the block with the neighborhood's mumbling, wandering bum. Buddy goes to fetch her back. The vagrant asks, "This your dog?" "Yes." "You can have her back for a quarter." The bum makes a quarter, and Sheila trots home with her human.

When I ask if Sheila has a dog house, Catfish responds, "A half million dollar house! She's cool when it's hot, hot when it's cool, gifts under the Christmas tree and daily big adventures." I sigh, thinking how this squat, troll-like mutt has the affections of over a dozen fine men and several devoted women. I don't think I would have gone "home" either.

Sheila

Saint Ginny of Long Island |

Philip Gonzales

Philip Gonzalez is one of those lucky people who find meaning in their work. As a hot-steam pipe fitter at Ellis Island and the World Trade Center, he takes great pride in his work. It affords him a luxurious life of travel and material goods. On one fateful day his comfortable existence comes to a complete end.

Philip's coat gets caught on a large metal stripping machine that is running full tilt. He awakes from a severe concussion with a destroyed writing arm, reconstructed jaw and cheek, and a career that is no longer his. His neighbor/friend, Sheilah Harris, is very concerned. Philip has not been outside for days; she knows he has hardly eaten. Sheilah decides the depressed man needs a dog. But Philip does not even want to take care of himself, let alone a dependent. I ask Phil, "Why didn't she suggest a self-sufficient companion, like a cat?" "Sheilah did not like cats."

Once the determined Sheilah gets Philip to the animal shelter, he decides to seek a pedigreed protective breed. In one run there are two dogs that have just been spayed. He chooses the Doberman, but Sheilah watches as a small wire-haired B&W dog comes forward to lick his hand. The mutt's entire being is directed toward the depressed man. With the encouragement both of Sheilah and the attendant, Philip agrees to take the unlikely candidate for a walk. They hobble outside into the sun and the dog stops. She looks up at him, her full face smiling, eyes sparkling. Yes, the rest is history. Philip Gonzalez's life is to change in unimaginable ways, and so is Sheilah's.

The schnauzer-husky-mix becomes Ginny. She had been found in a closet where she had been left for several days with her three pups. All have survived. Now, here she is in an apartment with an ocean view, a full-time person and another person that seems to love her just as much.

Out on one of their first walks, Ginny starts pulling and barking. Three men up ahead are kicking something about.

Ginny lunges at them. Dang, it's a cat! Phil yells at them to quit as he charges at them with his gimpy arm inside his leather jacket. Ginny breaks free to snap at their fleeing feet. With them gone, she tends to their victim by tenderly licking his bruises. The black cat is named Vogue and comes to live with Ginny and Phil. "Hey, I thought you didn't like cats?" "Ginny is very persuasive."

A couple of weeks later Ginny finds a newborn litter of kittens stuck down a pipe. The mother is nowhere in sight. At home the dog adopts the litter as hers, providing diligent grooming and constant nurturing while Philip and Sheilah bottle-feed them. When out on walks Ginny is on a mission: to help and befriend all cats. To date, the locations of Ginny's rescues include bushes, barbecue pits, the space under a shattered window, abandoned cars, garbage cans, a loading dock.

With Sheilah's old Ford filled with cat food and fresh water, every night the team visits nineteen cat colonies in the wee hours. They feed the hundreds of cats originally discovered by Ginny. Cats that are too shy to go up to Sheilah and Philip rub against Ginny and follow her everywhere. Sheilah has described the scene for me: "Silhouetted by a full moon, dozens of cats looking like diminutive horses gallop to greet and surround Ginny. This is Ginny in her glory. She does all the grooming and nuzzling to her heart's content. Philip and I spend our time filling bowls."

Philip first pays for the ever-expanding vet bills and pet food by selling off his collection of gold coins, his life savings. However, while I am at his

Sheilah Harris and cats

Ginny with Little Sheba

of this." She never finds any money; her heart isn't in it. The other two dogs she lives with, fellow foundlings, are very sweet, but not cat-rescuers. They show very little interest in the fifty plus cats in either apartment. There is a giant 28-pounder (not fat), another that has cerebellar hypoplasia, several that are blind, a tripod, two flat-faced Persians, and just about every coloring and marking you have ever seen.

Ginny has won Cat of the Year Award at the prestigious Westchester Cat Show and Heart of Gold Award through the Animal Medical Center. She has made several guest appearances on TV, and her story has been recounted in dozens of books, magazines and newspapers. Two books on her heroic feats have been published. When Ginny became world-renowned, a Japanese film crew set up a mock rescue on a loading dock. Ginny, of course, understood and quickly took off to the next loading dock where there was an actual cat in need.

I look at this elderly dog with her alert expression and kind eyes, surrounded by cats that take their turn to rub against her. I realize I am possibly beholding the greatest individual I have ever met. The Mother Theresa of cats. I ask Philip, "What happened to the two people that didn't like cats?" "They don't exist anymore. You know, Ginny's first rescue was me."

apartment numerous large bags of food appear. A little later two giant laundry bags arrive at Sheilah's: cat sleeping pads, cat wash cloths, cat towels. "We have become a non-profit, The Ginny Fund," explains Phil. "We now get great prices on food and discounted veterinary care, but still it never ends. At one time I got fed up and said NO, I can't do this! Ginny started to whine and cry. I asked her, 'Are you crazy? Do you know what this is costing me?' She did not stop making a racket till we were out the door and heading to her beloved cats."

One day Philip shows Ginny some money, trying to get her to sniff it as he implores her, "Make your next find some

Detail from Saint Ginny of Long Island

Saint Ginny of Long Island   32˝ x 28˝   Oil on board

Bordontown Buddies | This is my second time at By the Book in Bordonton, New Jersey, my all-time favorite place. Arlene's events have a lively following, including artists and writers; and although I am there tonight to give a talk and sign books, I'll be mutually entertained by this crew.

Folks are settling in to hear me talk about *Cat Book* when Mary shows up with pale-blond cocker Sandy. Sandy is delighted with any and all attention, and our oohing and aahing over her three-inch-long eyelashes. I mention being in the process of creating *Dog Book*.... "Oh! Sandy is available!" Yeah, but is she a rescue? "Absolutely! She was rescued from a pet store." That doesn't count. "Well, she couldn't stand up in the cage. She was so pitifully cramped I couldn't leave her there." Did you report the place? "No, but it closed down shortly thereafter."

When Bobbie, a local writer, announces, "I've got a Saint Bernard at home. I'll go get Kodiak." A rescue? "Yes, rescued from bad backyard breeders. The only thing filthier than poor Kodiak's surroundings were the people. It was gross. Believe me, we couldn't leave him there."

Bad pet stores and bad breeders. I can't stand people supporting either, but at least these two dogs were removed from objectionable situations. (Animal shelters do follow up on leads regarding animal welfare concerns and respect your need for anonymity. Also, multiple calls from different people and requests to know the outcome can lead to faster action.) Arlene suggests we meet up with Kodiak, the St.

Kodiak's Perfect Heart   8" x 10"   Graphite on paper

Bernard, at breakfast. Here at her shop the dog would make things very cramped.

The following morning Bobbie shows up with enormous Kodiak. On his side is a perfect huge heart (see drawing). Kodiak places his humongous head in my lap, letting me know he is really a lapdog. At his house I get to meet their guest, Sophie, a classic rescue: survivor of abuse, adopted from the shelter, mixed with every breed imaginable. She has been renamed by Bobbie's son "The Atomic Dog Made by Spasmatic." I am told she used to be really wound-up, but with the St. Bernard's mellow ways she has become more like him and she has livened him up. Sophie is here until her family, who are temporarily residing in an apartment, complete their dream house. They are getting back a greatly changed dog, with manners, although the dog that just jumped up on me appears to have a way to go. Once Ms. Spasmatic leaves, Kodiak's family plans to be a foster home for the St. Bernard/Newfoundland Rescue group. Evidently up North there is a need for this.

From Kodiak's home I head to Sandy's, the cocker with lashes. Sandy's mom Mary takes me to their backyard leading out to a field; a forest lies beyond. Sandy was rescued a second time, right here, by mostly feral cat Shedinski. Sandy and Mary were in this very field taking their daily stroll when one of the hunting dogs from down the street broke loose. The hound seems to view Sandy as prey as he tries to grab her out

Kodiak   12" x 12"   Oil on board

of Mary's arms. Mary steps on the attacking dog's chain, throwing Sandy as far as she can and yelling at her to run home. The small dog, transfixed, does not budge. Mary pulls the chain in the opposite direction from the way the attacker is lunging. She is dragged several yards when both she and the hound see Shedinski the cat spring out of the forest in full view. Mary untangles; dog with chain bounds after the cat, retreating deep into the woods. At home Mary falls to pieces. She and Sandy are intact, but what about this recently adopted, shy stray?! Dinner time arrives and so does Shedinski, the Hero!

Another successful trip to my favorite stop comes to a close. The difference is that when I return with the next book, they will be a part of it.

Sandy and Shedinski, the Hero Cat   16" x 14"   Oil on board

Retirement's Not So Bad | Despite this being a state

without organized betting, except on an Indian reservation, it is easy to find a greyhound because the greyhound network is the most organized and largest rescue organization for a specific breed. The job is huge. They work to place those thousands of dogs that come off the track, those that didn't make the cut, and those that have to be re-situated when a home does not work out. My subject today focuses mostly on the last category.

Brodie, a slight male, has a short career as a racer. Ken Culbreth suspects his companion combined a meekness that didn't permit aggressive competition and an independence that prevented his following the required rules of the game. "I believe he was jumped and traumatized by the other dogs. For Brodie that would be enough." The twelve-year-old brindle greets me most cordially. With that done, curiosity abated, he goes to stretch out on one of his bean-bag beds placed strategically throughout the house. "These dogs truly understand retirement and take it to the nth degree." Brodie is very beautiful and peaceful on his bed. At age twelve he is old for a greyhound and has survived pancreatic cancer, but appears to be very healthy and youthful in appearance despite a ghost face (the white associated with elderly dogs).

Brodie is whelped in Texas and races in Florida, but by age two and a half is turned into the Wake County SPCA by an elderly man saying he can't handle the high-spirited dog, and, by the looks of the malnourished greyhound, feed him either. This is Brodie's second or third home after coming off the tracks. Ken Culbreth, having just watched the National Geographic special on greyhounds and the plight of these retired racers, zooms over to see his first greyhound ever when the SPCA ad comes out featuring one. At home living with five ex-racers, Bob Brady, a major player in the greyhound network, is standing by to interview and talk with whoever might show an interest in the homeless dog. Ken points out there appears to be zero chemistry between him and the subject. Bob explains that in the animal's current situation he can hardly be expected to shine. Ken decides to make the commitment.

Brodie blossoms quickly into a self-assured individual and gains much-needed weight. Through their shared respect for the breed, Bob and Ken become allies in helping retired greyhounds. When Bob Brady dies, the people he was networking with get together to officially form the Triangle Greyhound Society, thus guaranteeing that others will continue his work. Ken signs on as a foster home, and in very short

Brodie   34" x 24"   Oil on board

By the Sea   5" x 12"   Graphite on paper

order, accompanied by Brodie on weekends, they table at events and festivals, educating the public about these quiet dogs. Brodie works as an ambassador, greeting people. "In helping him to become more extroverted, I may have gone too far. He can be very enthusiastic in his role and overwhelm his new friends."

In addition to educating the public about how wonderful greyhounds are as companions and pets, the Triangle Greyhound Society readily accepts any homeless or abandoned greyhound and provides needed medical care and foster homes before relocating the dog in a permanent home. The local animal shelters contact them whenever a greyhound lands in one of their runs. The animal is then moved to a foster home if one is available. When a home has a vacancy and one of the local greyhound adoption groups has an overflow of dogs, group members will pick up one or more of the dogs and house them for a period of time. At any given time, some of the local groups can have as many as thirty or forty greyhounds awaiting placement. The source for these dogs is never-ending as racers are constantly being retired or simply haven't made the cut.

Ken states, "Our group can't take a stance pro or con racing. Instead, we focus on the wonderful and gentle temperament of the dogs and the fact that they make fantastic companions. Many of the tracks are glad to give dogs up to Greyhound Rescue. They want to see them live out their natural lives in great homes. This door must always remain open between the track and rescuers. The dogs count on it."

Brodie and Ken have just moved to their new home in central Raleigh. Empty boxes are still stacked outside and the yard is not fenced yet. I'd hoped to catch Brodie's graceful bounding and sprinting, but without a fence it is chancy. Ken takes off his leash, and indeed the dog sails easily around the yard, but then stops to notice the street. My heart is in my mouth. Ken calls his name, but Brodie ignores him and continues flying around the house. Ken calls insistently until slowly Brodie returns to him with a grin on his face and a glint of mischief in his eye.

I ask, "Did you train this dog at all?" "Yes, but only on recall. That was necessary and he still needs work on the command. He will knock you down to get outside to do his business, no training needed there. He arrived too stressed out to put him through intensive training. He is very much his own dog. I don't own him, I live with him." Does Brodie guard his home? "Absolutely not. If there was a break-in he'd go to the other side of the house. I have an alarm system for protection. That is not what you normally have a greyhound for. They are simply lovable fourty-mile-an-hour couch potatoes." Brodie has sprinted around the yard, made a halfhearted attempt to leave, and now wants back in. He curls up on a bed. This breed is a perfect apartment dog, great on a leash, still as a rug inside.

Ken has boxes of photos of greyhounds racing down the beach, greyhounds at the beach house sacked out, draped all over each other, greyhounds in parades with hats, coats, bow ties. "Hey, isn't that Brodie in the antlers?" "Yes, we are in two to four parades a year. He enjoys being on display. He loves a walk, a car ride. He eats well. Brodie gets no commercial dog food. I cook everything fresh for him with his vitamins mixed in." Whatever, it works. The dog looks amazing at age twelve. With his gentle temperament and quiet demeanor, he well exemplifies this beautiful breed.

Wolfhound Greta, As in Garbo |

Greta Standing
9" x 7"   Graphite on paper

In 1994 Jim is perusing the internet for his dream dog, a Russian wolfhound. He locates one in need of a home in Tennessee. He discovered the breed when reading *War and Peace* in a Russian literature class. The book's hunting scene portrays the hound as the truly noble, loyal, ethereal giants they are. Going to a breeder would never be an option for Jim or his wife Linda. They are a certified foster home for our local shelter and know the bleak statistics: 16,000 dogs euthanized daily in the United States. Yes, Jim will experience the companionship of this most majestic breed, but as a rescue.

Off they go to Knoxville, Tennessee. Vi-Anne, an ex-breeder who now does borzoi rescue, will be meeting Jim and Linda in a hotel parking lot. Her home is in the outlying countryside, and so this is more convenient. The dog she hopes to place today came from a breeder down in Atlanta, Georgia, who was going out of business. In addition to his neglectful care, he threatened to release all the dogs he had.

They meet on time. The Russian wolfhound steps out of Vi-Anne's vehicle, and Linda has to catch her breath. "I just wasn't prepared. She is so big and so beautiful and she is going home with us! I felt so honored." Linda strokes the dog's long, flowing fur as she is given a hound hug by the leaning borzoi. The ex-breeder is pleased. "I can tell you are the correct home by the way you touch her." It is a great sense of accomplishment when a homeless animal finds a great home in a less than perfect world. On the way home, as promised, they stop in Asheville at Linda's sister, Jonelle's, who has told her children they are dropping by with the new puppy. They must be gentle. Jaws drop when the 110-pound puppy emerges.

Greta   23" x 14"   Oil on board

Greta Sitting   6" x 9"   Graphite on paper

The newly adopted dog comes with eye liner. She reminds Linda and her sister Pam (see first story in *Cat Book*) of the legendary beauty of Greta Garbo. So Greta she is. Finding a Russian name is quickly forgotten.

For the first two months Greta is kept separate from the cats. J and L are told to be wary of her with smaller animals. Borzois have great reputations for hunting wolves, coyotes and anyone smaller, so for the time being the cats and the sub-dued giantess must view each other through the French doors. When the doors are open, there are sniffs all around but nothing to indicate any danger. In fact, over the next nine years many foster animals come and go, and Greta gets along with all perfectly. She is calm and gentle and hunting never occurs to her, or, as Jim puts it, "She hunts for treats and races to the couch." Her preferred place to lounge is on a couch, as it is easier to step onto than to go all the way down to the floor. Like their first cousin, the greyhound, the borzois are couch pota-toes. In addition to this basic disposition, Greta is eleven, ancient for a giant breed. I'm not anticipating much action.

Outside Greta's silky fur glistens in the sun; she heads for shade. This breed is most sensitive to heat. The backyard ends at another fenced yard, and Linda flings the adjoining gate open. In runs black Lab-mix Lucy. Greta comes to life; long bangs of flowing white mark her every move. The two bounce around the entire circumference of both properties, doing fig-ure-eights. The ole gal is spry! Not ten minutes later Lucy retreats to her yard and Greta lies down in the shade. The young Lab has adapted to this particular style of play, short spurts of energy, until the next time. Greta heads back to air conditioning. I watch as her tail flows just as Linda describes. "She's a tail waver, not a tail wagger."

A Wild Westerner Named Toto | Using frequent–flyer miles, I fly out to Washington state to see my good friend and ex-boss, Debra Dunn, and her dog companion, Toto. She hired me, an itinerant artist in the early 1980's, as a visiting artist. Together we painted the small town of LaGrande, Oregon, a multitude of colors.

Well, here we are, certainly older and perhaps wiser. Toto is a feisty, independent schnauzer/cocker mix trotting up ahead of us along the Columbia River. Deb tells me about one of her favorite ploys. "At night Toto tells me she has to go out for a last little bathroom call. Once out she heads up the

Toto From the Wild West   20" x 20"   Oil on board

greenway along the river. She empties all the cat food bowls placed at the back doors. She's a rascal and a true survivor. I'm her third home, third state, third name, and all that in just her first year and a half."

Together, their first home is in Richland, Washington, on fifty-five acres owned by Deb's parents. At the end, down a dirt road, are Deb's three acres. With all this land Toto will be able to roam freely as her new person goes to her job. First day of work after Toto's arrival, Deb starts to head out. In the rearview mirror she sees the small dog running full tilt after her. D stops. Did Toto believe she was being abandoned once more? Now Toto hops into the car, enroute to grandma's! At her mom's Deb explains the dilemma of having to leave Toto behind. Grandma is delighted to have her granddog's company. Deb is now able to head off. This routine works for everyone. Towards the end of the day Toto heads home, stopping to play in the field and waiting leisurely for Deb.

Toto

Back home Deb sees a fox running and Toto in swift pursuit. Then Toto takes the lead. Then the fox zooms ahead. It's an obvious game of tag. At the time, the dog's play date with the fox seems cute, but later D wonders if it all could have turned deadly. Toto enjoys unusual playmates. On another occasion, while Deb is horseback riding around the hills with her dad, Toto trails with the two Dalmatians. Looking back, no Toto. They loop around. Still no Toto. The crew return home; still no Toto. Deb and her father unsaddle and grain the horses. They then take the truck to find the missing canine. They park and go on foot, searching in opposite directions. Deb spots Toto halfway up the hill. She is not alone; she is playing with a coyote. "Fortunately the coyote appeared friendly and not hungry!"

Yet another time, while Deb was camping with her husband in a pup tent, Toto slept in the car for safety's sake. Thank Great Goddess, as in the wee hours a large elk came crashing through pursued by a pack of howling coyotes. Toto from within the car made her own racket, desperately wanting to join the chase. "I don't know that we could've held her back from bursting through the canvas!"

Toto is an athletic dog, as most dogs tend to be, but she has some special skills. She can see above the wheat fields by jumping four feet straight up. Her leap into the Toyota Tercel is nothing less than aerobatic. Toto and Deb once visit a friend whose home is surrounded by prickly brush. Toto is so engrossed with the smells and the adventure that when she picks up a thorn, she continues on three legs without slowing down. When she picks up a second thorn, she continues to lope along on just two legs!

Toto not only has close brushes with death, but with fame, too. Deb's mom enters a photo of herself and dog into a Joan Rivers Show contest. D is wearing Western gear, Toto a red bandana, both sitting on the old buckboard of the pioneer family's ranch. Spike, the Wonder Dog companion of Joan Rivers, writes back personally, "I love your photo. It is posted on the best dog wall in town." Deb is not surprised, as Toto, her own Wonder Dog, "looks like my favorite toy come to life!"

Buster, Bucky & Bitsy | Caroline returns from the island of Tortola, having seen a small dog she is enamored of. "I know now what kind of dog I want." "Oh, please," I say, "just go to the shelter and save a life!" "I'm willing to go there to see if they have my preferred breed. I'm now ready for a shih tzu to enter my life." Caroline doesn't have to wait long. A week later I'm driving over to her house when I see her breed of choice strolling down busy University Drive. I put the scraggly little

A World of Glamour   19"x 19"   Oil on board

Bucky

dog in my car and off we go to his potential new home. "Oooh, he is a mess," proclaims C. Anyway, whatever she may be thinking, I have to research where he hails from before he can be adopted.

The hobo-looking shih tzu is wearing a collar with only a rabies tag. Fortunately it is enough information to reconnect him with his folks. The tag number is local; in fact, registered with the Durham animal shelter; they have all the pertinent information on file. The dog is Buster. We contact the dog's people, and after I leave C's, the owner comes and picks Buster up. He explains to Caroline that his wife is very ill, and thus they have little time for the dog. C tells him she is interested in this breed and would gladly adopt him. A couple of days later he phones and asks if she is still interested. She

says ok, but is not entirely sure, as Buster is not at all like the warm, bubbly dog she met in The Islands.

She takes the lethargic dog to the vet's for a check-up and grooming. She receives back a changed Buster. He is delighted to see her and is almost spunky. The gunk around his eyes is gone, his coat looks all shiny and new. Daily eye drops will be a part of his life, but besides that he is in great shape for an eight-to-ten-year-old dog. He happily pokes around his new home, realizing his new person is very attentive. He learns quickly that he can now ask and receive.

Buster fills Caroline's arms perfectly. C feared the dog was aloof. Maybe he was, but since discovering the joys of being held, groomed and carried about, he is transformed. He softly grunts with contentment from the attention. C and B are a team. They are always together. Caroline declares, "Buster is the love of my life." Her sleeping disorder is solved as he happily sleeps in her arms.

Buster's best friend is a fellow shih tzu, Bucky, living just down the street. His family has just had a second child. With a shift in their priorities they ask Caroline if Buster would like a

Buster

Bitsy

their conversation someone brings in a stray shih tzu, whom Jill grooms gratis as she is a rescue. Enter the beautiful Bitsy with long long eyelashes.

Bitsy is the most gregarious dog imaginable. A neighbor offers to photograph her. She strikes a pose and holds it. A tilt of the head, a look backwards. She excels in obedience school as she absolutely loves the social aspect. For this reason Caroline makes her a Halloween outfit, a harem girl from 1001 Nights; Bucky is dressed as her love slave. Bitsy is thrilled to dress up, but Bucky hates it. Trick or Treating is her thing, not his, so Bucky turns around and goes directly home. However, this is the beginning of a journey into beauty and fashion for Bitsy.

At Cornwallis Road Animal Hospital, Bitsy wins a prize. The following year she wins as Miss Kitty from Gunsmoke, with Bucky a begrudging Matt Dillon. The third year, soloing, she takes first place as Bitsy Ross. As Carolyn states, "It is Bitsy Ross, not Betsy." She is given an "I VOTED" sticker during the controversial elections of 2000, and she attends the First Annual Tree Planting for the victims of 9/11. Since then there have been many photo shoots, fashion shows and a few benefits. Her wardrobe includes a yachting outfit, cocktail dress, Easter ensemble, many sun dresses, and of course, her famous hat collection. As she now flies to the Caribbean frequently, Caroline is sewing her a stewardess outfit. When I say this is all a bit much, Caroline points out, "Bitsy is not spoiled. If she were we would be flying first-class. We ride coach with the real people."

brother? C agrees; the two boys are like super glue. Bucky loves to be with other dogs. Buster still loves cuddling with Mom.

When winter comes she dresses Buster in one of his sweaters; Bucky will have nothing to do with it! Buster is getting old and appreciates the added warmth. Bucky doesn't. He protects the older dog. Caroline begins to face the fact that at some point the love of her life, Buster, will pass on. She does not know how either she or Bucky will deal with this. At Dog Stylists of Durham, she mentions her fear to the proprietor, Jill, who agrees that locating a third dog now would be best. Shortly after

Dog Class | For the first class through the Durham Parks and Recreation Department, we meet dogless at the Armory for orientation with instructors Linda and Jamie. Puppy class, beginners and advanced beginners are all grouped together. Correct collars, jumping up, chewing, aggression are mentioned. The choke collar is obsolete and dangerous, causing trachea damage, and worse. The pinch collar looks worse, but is a miraculous invention, as it stops the human's arm from being ripped from its socket. This I like.

China's excited. So many dogs to play with at once! Not my reason for being here, but certainly hers. Trudell, Lucy, Grover, and Skippy are all of the same mind-set: PARTY! PARTY! PARTY! Rachael is subdued and seems disdainful of the rowdy bunch. Jasmine, the biggest, with lavender tongue, will and does attack when provoked. Bentley is most under control with his eleven-year-old handler, Amanda. The other junior handler, Laurie, is also eleven, and her dog child, wits,Skippy, has been an *enfant terrible* at home. Her parents are close to their wits' end.

Ruth is shy and reserved and stays close to her human dad. She and her brother Cooper were found abandoned by the side of a road. Both are adopted by Richard, who is dedicated

Rachael – Most Elegant
9" x 7"   Oil on board

China – Class Instigator
9" x 7"   Oil on board

to seeing that the rest of their lives are as close to perfect as possible. Unfortunately Cooper can't take the class. His twisted basset-hound legs are healing from several corrective operations. The surgeries have been successful, but dog class would be too physically demanding.

Second class, Jasmine is now civil and understands the commands well. Ruth has her stubborn moments, but wants to please. Grover, all heart, rolls on her back—wiggle, wiggle, wiggle. She never takes class seriously. China only behaves

Dog Class   10" x 30"   Graphite on paper

Lucy – Class Clown
9" x 7"   Oil on board

Ruth – Daddy's Girl
9" x 7"   Oil on board

Skippy – Most Improved
9" x 7"   Oil on board

Bentley – Mama's Boy
9" x 7"   Oil on board

Grover – Love Puppy
9" x 7"   Oil on board

Jasmine – Best Coat & Tongue
9" x 7"   Oil on board

Trudel – Party Animal   9" x 7"   Oil on board

Rachael

when there are ample doggy treats. Otherwise, as with Lucy and Trudell, it's still PARTY! PARTY! PARTY! These girls LOVE coming to class and the motivating factor is socializing. Rachael is a little friendlier toward the wild bunch, but unlike them she remembers her humble beginnings. She was adopted through Doberman Rescue and shows her appreciation by being beautifully behaved at all times. The rowdy shelter mutts appear to have perfect amnesia that way.

Skippy and Bentley are doing great. Uplifting to behold are the bond and the understanding our young handlers display with their canine companions. This class does not offer knowledge that they can get from sitting in a classroom or watching TV. Laurie and Amanda know instinctively, in a compassionate and caring manner, how to be in control. Future leaders, they prove it here.

Last class, all heel, halt, sit, lie down, turn pretty well. Each dog student with student dog handler walks up in turn to receive a diploma. Fortunately we get ours before China decides she needs to bark loudly and continuously in celebration. As the other dogs start to join in, we beat a quick exit.

Sick Puppy, Good Kid

Sick Puppy, Good Kid | Sixteen-year-old Katie attends dog class with young Taylor. Sometimes they participate, often they just watch. Her mother, Linda Tilley, is the instructor. Taylor, a tawny-colored boxer mix, knows the drill, but due to his size and youth, Katie holds him back. Occasionally he yips to join in. He is highly socialized, but gets quickly tired because of the ordeal he recently lived through.

Katie lives with her mother and two sisters north of Durham, and also with ten dogs, seven cats, four goats, a couple of horses, and an untold number of chickens, guinea hens, and parakeets; and they own and operate a boarding kennel. The stray dogs they find are trained, then placed in good homes. Several they have kept because of a disability or character flaw. Their homing pigeons they would love to give away, but they would only return. Despite the crowd, Katie has a strong desire to choose and be chosen by a puppy that needs her specifically. She envisions a larger muscular breed and talks with a breeder of show boxers.

On a chance visit to Durham's APS, Katie views a solitary puppy curled up in a small bed, head comfortably hanging over to one side. In the visitor room the little guy comes alive. Leaping about grinning, he is delighted with Katie and she with the little wild one. If the deposit placed on him falls through, they will return for him. It does fall through, and

Katie & Taylor   24" x 16"   Oil on board

Taylor

the spunky little boy lands a place in the female–run household. This is a triumphant Tuesday as Taylor enters his new home, but by Thursday Katie notices the active puppy is less so, and by Friday he is not eating. On Saturday a friend that works as a vet tech tests Taylor for parvo; it turns out positive. At the emergency clinic he is tested again with the same dire results. Taylor is given subcutaneous fluids and antibiotics. He will have to stay there in the isolation room with another dog that has a much more advanced case, but this hardly sounds safe, so home they go with the sick puppy.

Middle daughter Shannon is infuriated to see Taylor return. Her companion dog Hannah is a Rottweiler, a breed that is particularly susceptible to parvo. Shannon is taking no chances; they move out to her grandmother's down the road. Meanwhile, younger sister Katie makes an isolation room out of the unfinished basement, equipping it with a Great Dane sized cage, heat lamp, TV and radio. The entire house is disinfected with parvocide. Katie's bedroom is doused several times over. The bags used for the sick dog's waste are wiped down. Going into the basement, Katie changes into coveralls and a smock. When she leaves she walks through a clorox bath and wipes down all exposed skin. This procedure Katie carefully follows six to eight times a day as she tends to Taylor with Nutri-cal and alternative medicines. After a week the canine patient is gaining strength and regaining his appetite. The next week he barks when he hears noise upstairs. The third week, on New Year's Eve, teenager with spunky puppy emerges from the basement to rejoin the family above. Linda Tilley is particularly pleased to get her kennel helper back for this busy season.

A year has passed with no reoccurrence. Taylor has made a full recovery. The middle sister returns from grandma's with Rottweiler Hannah, and the two dogs quickly become best friends. Despite all the strays that Katie brings home and socializes, trains and nurtures back to health, she had a great desire to seek out someone that needed her specifically. She chose very well, but without the superb care she rendered, this chapter would not have had a happy ending.

Gabby, one of the permanent crew
5" x 5" Graphite on paper

Rottie Rescue: A Lesson Learned | Dog Book is a
third of the way done when Elizabeth, accompanied by husband and child, walks into my Annual Open Studio. "I'm interested in your work. I have a Rottweiler and I work with Rottweiler Rescue." Sounds like I've got another subject.

At Elizabeth's house I sit on the carpet as Malstrom brings me his rubber ball to throw. I did not know that Rotties are hard-wired to fetch, but this guy certainly is. Over the living room mantel is a large acrylic of another Rottie. "Who is this?" I point. "Moose, we got him from a terrible situation. When he died I made a promise to help educate and save lives. Malstrom I got from a breeder." "What?" "Hey, I was just out of college. My first pet as an adult AND I was dating an idiot that insisted I only look at purebred dogs. And the internet was not what it is today." So Elizabeth goes to a pet store, where she takes a pet-matching test. Three of the breeds can't be found in this country, and the fourth, the Rottweiler, she is not interested in; that is, until she witnesses a young child crawling all over one. The dog's gentleness convinces her to purchase a Rottweiler.

Just an hour from her home she finds a breeder. "Oh yes, come on out. We happen to have two beautiful litters ready for adoption now." Out at the kennel she asks why the mother dog looks so sickly and thin. Liz is reassured that this is normal for a dog that just gave birth two months ago. The puppies are playful and scramble about tussling with each other and jumping into her lap. Elizabeth turns and sees that one sweet pup has crawled into her pocketbook and is sound asleep. She accepts this as fate, pays the fee, and gets the pedigree proof her boyfriend deems crucial.

Back home Malstrom is an exceptionally calm puppy, and by morning he is obviously very sick. He is unable to keep anything down. Blood is in his stool. Boyfriend in tow, Elizabeth rushes with the new pet to the vet's. Mal has parvo. At this advanced stage the breeders had to know they were selling a sick dog. They tell Elizabeth to bring the dog back for a replacement. Liz does not view that as an option. The veterinarian not only agrees, but states that Mal would not survive even a brief road trip. He cannot be moved. The breeder states, "Well, that is our offer."

The young animal is placed under 24-hour care, quarantined, and monitored around the clock. On the sixth day the couple are advised to come in to bid farewell. Donning full protective gear, including thick rubber gloves, they attempt to stroke the small limp body. The next day the call comes in; they are prepared to approve euthanasia. But no, Malstrom gets up, eats, and drinks some water. The fever is breaking. He is going to live.

Spirits lifting, Elizabeth attempts to deal with the breeder again, explaining she would prefer not to have to seek legal counsel. They come around to reimbursing for the vet bills and giving her the correct certification for little Malstrom. They had given her the paper work for the previous litter the same

Detail of Malstrom

dog had had just six months ago. "Having come through parvo and dealing with the callousness of a puppy mill, I am now seeking information. Hey! I admit I was young and ignorant. This is a great breed, but in the right hands." Liz throws the ball again for Mal. He does not appear to be getting tired.

I mention that, when I worked at the shelter, six Rottweilers were nabbed in a drug raid. They ranged from extremely aggressive to the mildest, shyest animal. "That's right. They seek their place in the hierarchy. They are pack dogs, and the cruelest thing is to have one isolated. They are not solitary at all." Mal is very much a team player, and we are ignoring him for a minute. He goes and visits the baby, giving a quick lick to his face. He doesn't bother McClain with the ball, knowing he can't throw it yet, but when he can Mal will train the child as he has his parents.

We go for a walk. Mal walks between us without a leash, and McClain is carried in a sling. A couple cross the road as we approach and ask if the dog bites? Does he fight? Liz points out that the perception of the breed is so bad that finding good homes is tough. "This breed does not do well alone. Actually no dog does, but Rottweilers want to be with their family 24/7, and they are not the best watch dogs either." Up ahead a group of joggers see Malstrom and make a quick right. If they only knew!

Back at the house we sit on the carpeted floor. Mal collapses mostly on Liz, partly on me. "Do you know anyone that would make a good home for a Rottweiler? We just busted a puppy mill in Asheville. Many of the dogs are still boarded with the area vets. Our foster homes are full, even doubled up. Finding permanent homes will take months, even years. They have all gone through temperament testing. Just excellent dogs in need of excellent permanent homes. Hey, could you tell your readers that if they know anyone planning to breed their Rottie, DON'T!"

Malstrom   40" x 30"   Oil on board

China's Other Family | Solid arrangements have to be made for China. For the first time she can't go with me. The most helpful neighbors with the cats appear to have zero interest in being helpful with what they perceive to be a high-maintenance beast. I don't know any kennel owners personally, so that does not feel like an option. China has been with me only four months. She can't go back into a cage. Finally a friend with a fenced yard for her dog says sure, but her housemate says no. I'm running out of ideas. As a feeling of desperation begins to take hold, I remember the extreme dog person, Dietrich von Haugwitz, married to the former animal shelter president, Eva. Seventeen years ago I'd been to vegetarian potlucks at their house. But not more than eight years ago, we protested in front of a store selling fur. OK, so it has been a while. I hope these German-born animal activists will remember me.

I phone them. They DO remember me! AND, "Sure, why not? Bring China over." Music to my ears! Just two miles from where we live, we head right over for a trial run. Out on their deck we meet Vincent, a polar-bear-looking dog who lumbers up, talking in a friendly manner. Playfully, China jumps on him and his pleasant voice changes to a growl. "I'm not in the mood for this now or ever." China understands and then jumps around with Mopsy, who is delighted to show her visitor the entire fenced yard. They race around. China leaps directly into the lily pond, scrambles out pulling plants with her, and runs directly into the house—boing!—and right up on the couch where she shakes off, mud and all. Perfect mud paw prints from carpet to couch. Oh, Great Goddess, let me die right now!

Vincent and Mopsy   30" x 24"   Oil on board

Dietrich becomes philosophical: "Ah, yes, well, this is what an alert, athletic young dog would do. I need to put up a temporary barrier around the pond." As I start to breathe again, I see Eva is not so amused; hands on hips, lips pursed, closer to a normal reaction, I'm afraid. "Eva, your husband sure is tolerant *(giggle, giggle, hint, hint)*." "Yah, he would be. The dog looks like his beloved Stanley." Dietrich elaborates. "Yes, Stanley. Stanley was the best friend I ever had. China has the identical coloring and markings. *(Good, she has done something right.)* Stanley was found in the woods, a lost puppy belonging to irresponsible neighbors. I think of him often. Molly, his sister, we eventually adopted too. But Stanley...so special."

Eva's special dog was Tanya. "For seventeen years she was a little satellite to me. Where I was, there the dachshund would be." And indeed, I felt something was missing with Eva. Could she feel temporarily like that about China?... Oh, no! China is once again amongst the lilies! Old Vincent howls like a Greek chorus: "Baaaad daaaawg, baaaad daaaawg!" Mopsy dances on the edge grinning, Dietrich runs to close the door, Eva looks exasperated. "So, when was this mutt born?" "March 10th." "No way! That's my birthday!" *(Ding! China has done something else right!)*

Dietrich is an expert barrier builder, and so the week goes well. On long hikes Mopsy chases sticks thrown into the New Hope River, and China chases Mopsy. Vincent mournfully complains, "Those two are obnoxious!"

We are returning to Eva and Dietrich's for their interview for this chapter. China is excited. She races ahead of me and waits impatiently for me to open their back door. She flies up the stairs, races to Dietrich, and plasters herself on top of him across the couch. Eva reminds her that she is here, too. Mopsy gives China an all-over face kiss. Vincent lifts his great white head and emits a low howl.

Eva and Dietrich are coming back from making a delivery to the Durham Rescue Mission when they find Mopsy. "There was this quivering dog a week before Christmas, in the middle of the traffic loop at rush hour. We swung back around and I jumped out and grabbed her." "And what kind of dog is she?" "She is a typical little *promenade michung*." "Oh, sounds fancy." "In English that means *Heinz 57*. She is very selective with her friends. We conclude she has had some bad experiences." Mopsy dances with teddy bear. She throws it up in the air, catches it,

swings it about, and if China is here, then tug-of-war happens. "Don't worry, I get the teddies from the Goodwill Store." And indeed, there is a pile of these once-cute bears.

When Vincent is adopted a decade ago, he reminds Dietrich of Polly, his first dog back in Germany. She escaped with them when the Russians invaded in 1945. The family is in hiding, and Polly has to be placed in more secure quarters. (Further details can be found in Charles Patterson's *Eternal Treblinka*, Chapter eight.) Nearly half a century later, when Vincent, the Polly look-alike, puts his paw out to Dietrich, he is taken back to those earlier times, and Vincent is adopted on the spot.

"I wasn't always an expert fence builder. Vincent here gave me cause." Until the great polar-bear dog arrives, E and D provide a happy safe home for a dozen white, pink-eyed, ex-lab rabbits. Stanley and sister Molly co-exist peacefully with them, but as a young dog Vinnie sees them as prey. After a fenced area proves little protection, the ten remaining albinos are whisked away to a refuge in South Carolina. Without the rabbits, Vinnie turns to the neighbor's chickens. The neighbor requests a donation be made to the shelter in honor of her dead birds and the fence secured. Dietrich provides both. On one side of the doctored fence are steps for the cat Mootz to enter and exit the yard gracefully. The large orange tabby is impervious to dogs and is more tolerant of China than the ever-complaining Vincent.

I tell E and D I'm giving them a painting of Vincent, Mopsy, the pond, etc.... "Oh, no, you can't possibly!" Eva protests, smiling, while Dietrich asks the size so he can start to figure out where it will hang. I'm wondering if maybe this is a very good time to tell them China is coming to stay for a month. Is the lily pond secure yet?

The Dogs of 9/11 | My parents, sister, niece, and aunts all live in NYC, so it is only a matter of months after 9/11 before I go to visit Ground Zero. Visitors, relatives seek a view from the platform constructed for this purpose, but the emptiness and the transformation are too huge for understanding, too intense for any comprehensible emotion. We gaze at a skeleton of misshapened beams pointed in all directions. Seagulls circle overhead. Cranes lift enormous fragments onto waiting platform trucks. The stench wafts uptown, but here it is heavier and more uniform.

Carefully combing through the mountainous chaos are the German-shepherd K-9s of the New York Police Department. All the original SAR (Search and Rescue) dogs working with them, some 350 canines of every breed and mix, have now gone home. Their initial rescue effort has spanned the first five days following 9/11, and then a month after that as they and volunteers from fifty states search around the clock for human remains. For twelve hours daily the dogs toil without respiratory, foot or eye protection, unlike their human counterparts. Foot wear can compromise their toe-splaying grip on unstable surfaces, and gas masks defeat the purpose of finding remains.

At the end of their shifts a veterinarian checks them over, administering subcutaneous fluids as needed, rinsing out eyes, inspecting all four pads and in between toes for shard cuts, listening to heart and lungs for damage from possible chemical inhalation, and then rubs them

At the Pile I 9" x 7" Oil on board

down. As survivors are no longer being found, they can become discouraged. To lift their spirits, live people hide so that when they are "found," the dogs can be rewarded with praise and hugs. All

At the Pile II   9" x 7"   Oil on board

I visit the K–9 Center in Brooklyn. Officer Chris Hanley releases out of a tank-like truck K–9 Kiefer. The wiry German shepherd bounces out. "Okay, what are we up to now?" his enthusiastic being asks. Kiefer is back in full form! The burdensome days at Ground Zero zapped his spirit...temporarily. His handler, Officer Hanley, has worked hour after hour, day after day, week after week, month after month, to motivate and inspire Kiefer to use all his resources to find remains. There are thirty-two such highly trained canines from the Brooklyn department working at the pile at any given time, 24/7.

"It's astounding where Kiefer goes, places where even the smallest human can't fit. A steel beam gets lifted, a new void's uncovered. Kiefer uses all his training, and then some. Dogs have to be kept motivated. As time goes on the scents get fainter. We have a cadaver smell and we plant an object dabbed in it. The K–9 finds it, gets praise and wants to continue his work. Twelve to fourteen hours of this each day. Long days. In the beginning there is so much cadaver scent, it's hard for Kiefer to figure out which direction to go first. The days pass and retrieval becomes less. Hopefully, though, each find will help us identify someone." "Does any day stand out?" "No, they were all long."

We enter the training course. Kiefer is anxious to get started. Officer Hanley unleashes him and off he goes. He leaps onto the balancing beam, trots along, jumps down, looks back at his handler. We follow Kiefer around the course. He is now sailing over hurdles three feet high.

I learn that all of the dogs are from the Czech Republic and Hungary. The fee is less and they are more genetically diverse. This last bit of information is very believable. On a wall

dogs survive the incredibly demanding work. Sirius, however, the World Trade Center bomb-sniffing dog, is down below when the first plane hits. His handler, Officer Lim, goes to investigate and debris covers him. Fortunately he is pulled out, but Sirius doesn't make it.

K-9 Kieffer and Officer Hanley
9" x 7"   Oil on board

in the main office there are 8" x 10" photos of each of the thir-ty-two canines with handler. Kiefer bounces over and poses perfectly. When I put my camera down, he gives me an all-over facial slurp. Like all dogs in this division, he is dual-trained, both in recovery and apprehension. At home he plays in a large fenced yard with Dakota, a spayed female shepherd. All the dogs in Kiefer's department are male. At work the dogs do not mingle, as it would be counter-produc-tive because they need to be fully focused on the task and their handler.

During that first month the dogs discover over 20,000 DNA-valuable parts that humans on their own would never find. After a month both the veterinarians and FEMA call off the searching by the volunteer SAR units—too many unwar-ranted hazards. When the 350 SAR dogs leave after their intense effort of more than a month, there is an additional sadness. It is hard to face, but New York's K-9 division has ten more lonely months at the pile. By the time they are done many thousands more body parts will have been found, and just about every person identified who died on 9/11 was done so through DNA analysis. For those missing loved ones the resulting information can be priceless and perhaps assist in the process of healing.

After 9/11 | Returning from New York, where I interviewed Officer Hanley and met K-9 Kiefer, I feel I understand only a very small part of what these dogs do. Those that worked on the 9/11 recovery process are too close to the effort and are understandably still recovering. Back home I find the website CSAR.com (Canine Search and Rescue) and write a general email inquiring about SAR dogs here in the South. Carolyn Knapp responds from Missouri. The black Lab–shar–pei–mix known as Digger and handler Max Bradburn come foremost to mind as a true dynamic duo. Mr. Bradburn has recently led a workshop at the Canine Academy at Camp Attabury in Indiana. While there, he worked with the German shepherds and officers of the NYPD Canine Department to help restore morale and thus return all fully into the game. The class participants had endured eleven months at Ground Zero.

Max and Digger live in Asheville five hours west of me. Fortunately I am scheduled to do an event at Malaprop's Bookstore only ten minutes from their home. After the thruway and a few twists and turns, I'm on their dirt road. Looking west or east, I see mountains, north or south forests, straight ahead seven dogs. China–dog is with me. I explain to

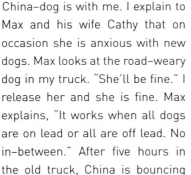

Shannon and Buddy

Max and his wife Cathy that on occasion she is anxious with new dogs. Max looks at the road–weary dog in my truck. "She'll be fine." I release her and she is fine. Max explains, "It works when all dogs are on lead or all are off lead. No in–between." After five hours in the old truck, China is bouncing about, friendly, sniffing all around.

Digger is a fit, muscular, black–velvet–coated mix with an alert expression. His handler, Max, who works as a volunteer fireman and has formed the HAZMAT team for the Blue Ridge Paper Company,

has been on countless rescue efforts. Once a toddler crawls into a brush pile and none of the SAR dogs are slight enough to enter in order to lead the child out. Fortunately at daybreak the child does manage on her own to wander out, but Max decides he'd best find a dog able to cope with tight, small spaces.

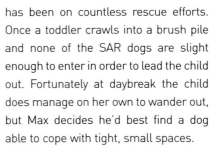

Cathy and Max

At the shelter Max and Cathy search for a Jack Russell-mix. They keep coming back to the puppy standing at attention, attuned to their every move, every sound, every smell. Nothing escapes him. Neither has seen anything like him. They leave thinking of the alert puppy; unfortunately he isn't a Jack Russell–cross. A week later Cathy announces, "If you're not adopting him, I am." Her husband returns just in time, as the dog's allotted moments at the shelter have nearly run out. I ask, "So did he take to training?" Max responds, "I taught him everything I know in half an hour; he's still teaching me." Digger turns out to be the perfect SAR canine. If there is someone to be found, he will find him.

With Shannon, Cathy's seven-year-old daughter, and eight dogs, we walk up the hill. Shannon is a sturdy child used to long hikes, dogs and Max's accounts of many, many rescues. At the top of the hill Digger stands still, nose up, breathing through his mouth, mouth slightly open. He is tasting the air, getting a more complete picture of a smell he has picked up. This is referred to as winding. He pops his jaw as he tastes the air. When it's hot and dry out he'll turn over leaves to further pick up a scent. Digger tracks his subjects primarily by air currents, unlike a tracking–and–trailing dog with nose to the ground following every footstep. An air-scent dog goes straight as an arrow to the source.

Shining Rock Wilderness Area, Great Smoky Mountains, Grandfather Mountain, Nantahala National Forest are all in the region—plenty of space for hikers to get lost. Digger is given a scent with the command "Scent." Then the instructions "Find the man," which indicates a live search, or "Find Fred" for a cadaver. When an inebriated man drowns trying to swim to a spit of land, Digger is quickly able to locate the approximate location by the gasses being released from the body under water. The area is dragged, the body found.

In another instance, a young man, having gone into the Shining Rock Wilderness Area to find himself, has instead become lost. Digger picks up his scent within 100 yards into the search, but it takes two days to reach the subject eight miles away. Another happy ending occurs with an older hiker reported missing for eighteen hours by his wife. With three bloodhounds and five air-scent dogs of various breeds, the man is quickly located first by Digger, but once all are on the scent it is very much a group effort. Around four in the morning they reach the elderly hiker, who totally denies being lost, but Max tells me he's never seen anyone happier to have been found.

On a lighter note, Digger and Tanner, one of the Jack Russells on the premises, work as a mischievous team. Digger stands in the middle of the trail staring down a hiker. When the hiker is respectfully still, Tanner sneaks around back and nips the victim in the rear. They pull this act on a frequent hiker who asks Max, "Do your dogs have their shots?" "Yes, why?" The stoic man turns around to reveal Tanner attached to the seat of his pants, little body dangling, big teeth implanted firmly into cloth. No wonder this creature is never taken on searches. Never.

When Digger's collar with bell for locating

Digger with Family   23" x 16"   Oil on board

China

his whereabouts is placed on him, he understands he is now in work mode. Geared up and given the scent, he is agitated, his total being on a mission, whether the command is "Find the Man" or "Find Fred." When he finds the live person, he runs to Max. "Treat and adoration time!" Digger demands. But when he finds "Fred," a cadaver, he contacts Max and then loses all interest. He will not accept his treat. Another great difference in the two search modes is that when Digger is tracking a cadaver, he drools and froths at the mouth, his nose pouring. None of these symptoms occur when the search is for a live person. I ask if he ever barks to signify a find? "Absolutely not. Should a relative of the deceased be nearby, it could be very disturbing. Once, though, Digger did bark, as it wasn't clear I got his meaning."

Every Tuesday the SAR dogs meet for training at different locations; each one goes in turn. For example, one evening at a schoolyard Digger, wearing his belled collar, is given a smell. Handler Max is not clued into any of the particulars. Digger takes off to find the student around the back of the building and returns all animated, but he won't accept his treat. The search is not finished. Then he tears off to the playground, climbs up the tower, over to the rope swing to the second student. He still won't accept his treat; instead he dashes off into the woods and finds the third youth. NOW he'll accept his treat! The scents of all three participants were on the card, with all three found in less than twelve minutes.

A big part of Digger's success is motivation. Max is tops at motivating and encouraging the dog. Together they make a powerful team. In helping police officers and their canines to recover, Max emphasizes very physical tussling, frisking and playing, not unlike wolf pups. "They arrive with that 1000-yard stare, simply burnt out, no attention span, no interest in food, nothing feeling good. It was great to see them turn around.

What they'd been through was unimaginably brutal."

China is exhausted. We've been fed a delectable dinner. Before I leave, Shannon insists on showing me her rope swing. It's hung from a branch twenty feet up, giving a huge radial ride. I'm tempted to try it, but like China, I'm exhausted. All this is a lot to take in.

Digger

Rasta Lipman-Preble-Anderson | Kimberly Preble is driving north to Connecticut, visiting family. She decides that Rasta, the canine companion of her Jamaican boyfriend Jahson Lipman, would make a good traveling buddy. "Can she go with me?" The boyfriend agrees, knowing the red-haired dachshund's love of road trips. Besides, these days, Jahson's work schedule has not been easy on Rasta. Too much time spent alone. Rasta is estatic. Every day a new adventure!

The long-haired dachshund is a hit in Connecticut. Everywhere she goes she is greatly admired. Back in Durham, Jahson's schedule is so frantic that Rasta stays a few days longer, just long enough for Kimberly's housemate Dena to fall madly in love with the dog. Wanting only the best for her, Jahson agrees that Rasta can stay. He reflects a little painfully: just a few weeks earlier, as he was walking in Manhattan, a stranger offered him $1000 for the small beauty. He refused the person's pleas, and now here he is giving her away for free. Love is like that, Jahson reflects.

Rasta still sees Jahson frequently, but now she has cats to groom (when they let her), as well as weekends at Kimberly's lake house, car rides all day as her human mom, Kimberly, does home health visits, and of course, road trips to Connecticut. When Dena moves out, in moves a very tall man, Terry Anderson. Dog and man become nearly inseparable. Kimberly confesses to me that she is a little put out by the affection Rasta is showing him. Terry goes on three-hour hikes and Rasta keeps up with him every bit of the way.

After Terry moves out, he observes a schedule with Rasta and gets permission to take her on his travels to Ohio, Maryland and Florida. He comes upon a breeder of long-haired dachsunds and passes the number on to Kim, suggesting she get herself another dog, implying Rasta was now with

Rasta with Copper and Sierra   22" x 18"   Oil on board

him. Kim is incensed and decides to rotate her work shifts so she can win the dog's affections back. What helps is that when she finds the young cat Sierra, Rasta now focuses on grooming this new highly tolerant animal. Terry is still here for fabulous hikes, Jahson still dotes on her, Kim caters to her every whim, and best of all, her Sierra cat understands that a dog must groom.

An Unlikely Pair | Mary Ellen's children left for college a

Mary Ellen

couple of years ago, and now her husband is threatening to move out. Not wanting to waste time, Mary Ellen explains to her land-lady that her husband is leaving—she needs a dog. Permission granted, she goes directly to the Durham Animal Shelter. Amongst the three long aisles of caged runs sits a miser-able little beagle named Spunky. She is off a farm, just a year old, but with keeled chest and short legs, she isn't a breeding speciman or a hunter. She is the picture of lonely. Mary Ellen can relate.

RHO, the place where Mary Ellen works, is a pharmaceu-tical research company, and for this reason the Shelter employee is reluctant to let Spunky go with this seemingly nice lady. Beagles have been the dog of choice to be burned, intox-icated, overdosed, electrified by preclinical research firms.

Samantha

RHO is a clinical firm, mean-ing their subjects are human volunteers, but some of their data is gotten from the other kind. After a home visit by Shelter staff, it is determined that Mary Ellen is not a vivi-sectionist and the beagle will be safe.

A fenced oblong pond sits at the end of the yard, along with a large dog house, cat-tails, frogs, fish, and more frogs. This will be Spunky's, now renamed Samantha's, yard. Exploring the great yard is fun, but Sam misses the company of other hounds.

Monkey

Mary Ellen she loves, but her husband...why is he still here? Sam steals his food and urinates by his chair, but otherwise they both ignore each other. Finally the husband moves out and Sam seems happier but still lonely.

When I go to see artist Lisa Creed, various mongrels dash to the fence. A little one with cat ears and a silly grin is leap-ing up. "Look at me! Look at me!" She is wiggling all over, her long tongue washing my hands, face, any and all exposed skin. "What's with this wildly affectionate dog?" I ask Lisa. "You cer-tainly have a crew!" An entire litter of adolescent dogs, it seems, has been found by a road. They are all thick-coated, short-legged, perky-eared characters. Monkey is what the lit-tle nutty hypercreature is called. Her brother, Henry, is unde-manding and calm. Their other siblings have stayed with the original person that found them. The rest here have lived with Lisa for years. Monkey is obviously not getting the attention she needs.

Mary Ellen agrees to take Lisa Creed's phone number. At the pond a week later I am being attacked by the love bullet named Monkey. Samantha is no longer lonely. She is mad! Monkey wants everyone's love and attention all the time. Sam is cool and aloof and has pride in her sedate but friendly manner. How is a classy girl to get any attention with a hyperactive flirt around? Sam chases Monkey away. Monkey spins around and chases her back, they tussle and rumble about. When Mary Ellen comes home they get treats, but Monkey needs fifteen minutes of hugs first. Sam slumps into her bed and looks on in disgust.

They have now been together several years. Monkey is still the extrovert, giving gifts to humans of things she doesn't want and bringing the dog in the mirror her toys to play with. She remains a flirt, but the desperation is gone. Samantha has learned from her and is no longer content with the occasional pat on the head. Instead she is now up on the couch in your lap, insisting that you look into her Cleopatra eyes.

Sam and Monkey at the Pond   23" x 16"   Oil on board

At the Brink | Tuesday morning and the museum is not yet open, nor is it sweltering yet. I'm alone with "the Family." Val has kindly turned the viewing monitor on early. Presently it is not needed. Both parent wolves have come up to the fence to sniff me and then the air. A couple of leggy pups join them. The dad lopes back to the den sixty feet away, jumping up to his perch on the roof. He howls in his mate's direction. She ignores him, sits down, stretches, yawns in my direction. Two pups relax by her side. She rolls over, paws dangling in mid-air and looks at me from her upside-down position with an angelic smile. I am totally honored. What a beautiful Tuesday morning!

Red Wolf Family
8.5" x 9.5"   Oil on board

The Museum of Life and Science is part of the Red Wolf Recovery Plan, so this second litter is a huge triumph. When the program was started, the red wolf was on the brink of extinction, with only nineteen left. Through very careful breeding, potentially suitable mates are paired and switched around to keep the gene pool as diverse as possible. Currently there are 250 red wolves, the majority in captivity, some released in wilderness areas. Three major factors have placed the breed in peril: loss of habitat, hunting, and mating with coyotes.

The school buses arrive, ending my solitary visit with red wolves. I'm not having a particularily easy time painting them anyway, but it is wonderful being so close to a creature so wild. Years ago I placed two red wolves in a mural I did on endangered species. Fast forward, the Raleigh Arts Commission sponsored the Red Wolf Ramble, fiber glass forms decorated by local artists. Some sponsors keep their wolf statues while others are donated for auction, raising more money for the arts.

Somehow the deadline to enter the Red Wolf Ramble slipped by me, so on my own I phoned businesses, doctors, and so forth, and asked them to get in on this exciting project. I was ignored until I mentioned the opportunity to my friends Karin and David. They had just built a palace, so appropriately they chose from my three wolf images the Palace Wolf design.

The near extinction of a breed is a sign that we are seriously out of balance. More large tracts of land need to be donated to land conservancy organizations, and you can help today by adopting a red wolf through any participating museum, zoo, or wildlife preserve.

Red Wolf Family at the Mueum of Life and Science
8.5" x 8.5"   Oil on board

Palace Wolf   Acrylic on fiber glass
Photo by David Jessee

Submitted ideas for the
Raleigh Red Wolf Ramble.

A Dog's Best Friend | At Digital Printing I am to meet up with Crazy Dog Man, David Sherman. He springs in, tousle-haired, with three dogs—there are never less accompanying him. He's wearing his standard uniform of khaki shorts and nondescript T-shirt, and although quite handsome, he has that never-looks-in-a-mirror style. "I've always done dog rescue, but a good place to start is the trailer park..."

David and wife Diane move into the Cole Park Trailer Park in the mid-eighties. There is a two-dog limit, so in the beginning they are careful their foundlings do not number much over the limit—maybe six to eight strays which they actively seek good permanent homes for. The landlord quickly catches on. He understands that they are running an unofficial shelter at the Park. He gives them permission to have as many dogs as they like as long as there are no complaints. More pens go up. Dogs are found abandoned on highways; friends find dogs in need and bring them to David and Diane. When there is a vacancy David goes to the Chatham County Shelter and adopts a couple that don't have a chance.

"My soulmate dog was Hogan. He was a formidable athlete, mostly malamute, some wolf, lightning fast. Skip a few frames and he is there. Tied up and asleep, he catches a squirrel. Walking through the woods, he is perfectly silent. Hogan likes sitting on the top of cars. So the roofs of ours are all slightly bowed in from his weight. I witnessed as a Pomeranian ran through our field. Two Rotties took after the small dog from the other side. I unhooked Hogan. In a flash he was standing protectively over the Pomeranian. The two large dogs turned away; they knew better than to mess with Hogan. He had such presence. I could go anywhere with him; restaurants, malls, and guards all made an exception for him.

Hogan   9" x 12"   Graphite on paper

Strangely, I grieve him the least. His presence is so huge he's still here. When I go to the Grand Canyon or see a fabulous sunset, he is there. He inspires grandeur. I am just privileged to have been with him."

A decade after the unofficial shelter began, the trailer park is sold to make way for a strip mall. Diane and David separate. David has to disassemble eight dog runs and relocate twenty-eight dogs to a safe zone. He camps out in a field with them in his Chevy wagon. They are evicted. Meanwhile, bulldozers reshape their former home, ignoring the graves of a dozen dogs. With those he has not adopted out, David turns to his childhood home in Michigan. There he finds a cabin to rent, but he receives notice. The local pound is after him with his seventeen dogs; they hide out in the woods. The winter is harsh, twenty degrees below. Placing as many as possible, he

David's Constant Threesome   26" x 23.5"   Oil on board

Yvonne

Dacs

heads back to North Carolina with only ten. Howard, his good friend, gives him a field to park in, stake out dogs, and put up pens. "This is a really comfortable setup. The old Dodge van holds about ten in their night-time crates. In the Chevy, five or six stay with me. Several prefer to stay outside." I ask him how he determines who stays in which vehicle. "The level of being housebroken. This has worked out beautifully. Mornings I go to my friend Michael's and get a great shower. Everything at Michael's is so meticulous, a real sanctuary. I love it."

I ask him to tell me about the three dogs who are with him. "Yvonne is a border collie-mix. She was brought to Diane and me by a homeless woman who found her starved and with a bloody raw neck where a rope had burned into her flesh. She is fiercely loyal to me and I to her. Dacs was pulled out from under a chicken coop. I rode out with the dog catcher on a complaint about a farm with many feral neglected dogs. Dacs was in such bad shape the pound official simply let me take her. I guess she's a dachshund-terrier. We didn't know she was pregnant. Fortunately, the litter was small and they placed easily." The third dog, Cody, like Yvonne, is a border collie-mix and well behaved in public. Consequently, he gets to go just about everywhere David goes.

While camping out on Howard's property and sifting through some photographs, David decides he wants a better quality image of his beloved Hogan. Julie's print shop is suggested as the best. David meets cat-rescuer Julie Smith. She has just spent a week at Best Friends, the famous Utah animal sanctuary, learning how to set up a no-kill shelter. Julie's shop becomes a place he visits frequently; she understands every nuance of animal rescue, helping David with parvo puppies, placing a Great Dane-mix and an English spaniel. She adopts two young dogs from him, but that's now a fuzzy line, as they've joined forces. Julie has just bought a 3,000-square-foot facility, and they have applied for their nonprofit status. Oak Grove Animal Sanctuary is now underway.

I look at this youthful, springy, disheveled man named David Sherman who lives purely through heart. "David, how old are you?" "I'll be sixty soon." Clearly he has found the secret to eternal youth and happiness.

Cody

Nikolai: *Russian for Sweetness* |

A visitor to my studio tells me of his wolf hybrid adopted from the Gastineau Humane Society in Juneau, Alaska. I am pleased as I envision the rescue being a necessary addition to *Dog Book*. All the hybrids I know of have been bred to produce more puppies, and I am not interested in rewarding or advertising either breeders or buyers. This hybrid is different....

Bruce agrees that Nikolai would be a great addition and offers to sprint to his car for his constant companion. Knowing what I do of some hybrids, I ask how he is with other dogs. "Never a problem." As he goes to get the hybrid, I tell China-dog, "You better behave now. Don't go getting dominant with a wolf!"

Enter Nikolai! The dogs need no introduction as they instantly enter gentle play–mode. The mellow giant was found in the wilderness of Alaska and named after a town on the Iditarod Trail, an annual dog–sled marathon. Roma–cat is coming down the stairs. His reason for introducing himself to new dogs is to put them in their place. The wolf hybrids I knew killed the family cat even though they were raised together. I tell Roma to go back upstairs. He refuses. The black alpha cat is perched at eye level with Nik. Nik gives his would-be torturer a swift kiss and returns to playing with China. Seems his companion at home is Savanna, a gray cat from the same Alaskan shelter where Bruce served on the board. Roma never scolds the visitor, absolutely no need.

Nikolai at the Eno River State Park   29.5" x 23"   Oil on board

Nikolai

When Bruce's daughter shows up with a puppy, Nikolai astounds one and all. He not only shares toys but places them in the young one's mouth, bringing him sticks to chew on and toys to play with. When the pup is insecure about descending the stairs, Nik helps him with gentle nudges. This dog defies all that I know about hybrids needing very adept handlers, so I phone someone who has bred German shepherd–wolf hybrids and who personally knows Nik. Norma currently has twelve hybrids. Her theory about Nik is that his percentage of wolf is low and he gets enormous amounts of socialization. She is right about Nik's social life. He goes to work with Bruce, runs in Duke Forest four times a week, on weekends plays with

up to thirty–five dogs in the dog park, enjoys trips to the beach and mountains, and never has a problem with another beast. Yet, as to where he was found, the percentage of wolf could be very high, but then his flop–over ears and remarkably sweet temperament? Could a hound dog have gotten into the mix?

Kaya, a dog rescuer, tells me of the wolf hybrid she got from a New York City shelter. She has to be on guard to keep him from attacking someone every ten feet. Bruce is fortunate with Nikolai as he has one of the easiest, sweetest dogs in the world. But what the heck was an unaltered hound-dog-mix doing up in a freezing tundra of Alaska?

Gremlin & Goddess | Dad and I are walking down Broadway when the smallest Pomeranian I've ever seen catches my eye. She licks my hand and cuddles close to me as I pick her up. Rosalind Harris, Tzeitel of *Fiddler on the Roof* film fame, is little Venus's latest home. A month ago she follows a child to her piano lesson, is passed on to a dentist, then to a friend of Roz, and now Roz says to me, "You're good with her. If I can't keep her, would you consider taking her?" I have visions of Roma-cat devouring tiny Venus, but before I can answer, Roz says, "No? Okay, I'll put you on the list should something happen to me. This sweet girl is my dream dog

come true. My other one, Phoenix, is a gremlin, a pit bull in a papillon's body! He pees doing a handstand, trying to get higher than the Great Danes!"

Agreeing to be in the book, Roz now starts mentioning her turtles, the Solomon Island tree skink Fred, the iguana Sol Soleil, and her beloved talking parakeet Bosley, who once, upon receiving a shot, told a veterinarian, "Stop that, bitch!" Roz swears she did not teach the bird that expression, or others, such as, "You're the greatest star." Or, "Hello, Gorgeous." Or, as she heads out to her flea-market booth, "Make some money." The tiny bird also learned the

Roz with Companions   24" x 36"   Oil onboard

lyrics to all her songs. When Bosley dies, Roz goes into deep mourning.

Mom and I visit Roz and Venus at her flea-market booth, where she sells estate jewelry between shows. Both human and Pomeranian are impeccably groomed. It is one of those miserable scorchers of a day, so I make plans to meet her the next day at her place.

Bosley

I'm expecting back-alley funk, a wild aromatic blend from floor to ceiling of eau d'iguana, turtle, skink, dog, and bird. Almost the total opposite, with no clutter or smell. The divinely feminine, borderline-opulent apartment is pristine. The gremlin-dog Phoenix presents me with a ball to throw and won't stop yapping until I fulfill his continuous command. Evidently he has the ball-retrieving gene hot-wired into him; not just a miniature pit bull but a five-and-a-half-pound retriever, too! Venus is delighted to see me again. Roz

expounds on how perfectly behaved she is at the flea market, absolutely the dog she has waited for all her life. If the original "owners" spotted the "found" ads now, it would be too late. Venus is in her permanent home.

Pheonix

When Roz first met the domineering papillon Phoenix, he was being carted around in a red wagon like the little biting prince he was. "This was the first time I met a dog I didn't like." Even with being very clear about her sentiments, when Phoenix's human slave passes away, the responsibility of the little demon rests solely on Roz. "The placement was a temporary thing. Every day was a trial. There were times I couldn't get near my bed. He'd run back and forth growling and snapping, literally possessing my bed. He bit if I tried to touch him." With the help of an animal behaviorist, they settled into a life together.

Roz shows me the other residents. Venus loves all of them. Phoenix is now annoyed—too much attention lavished on others. He growls, lip curled; an evil look and stance come over him. He is thinking about having a full-out temper tantrum, but instead turns it off and reluctantly allows me, after I've been here for three hours, to pet him and acknowledge his divine beauty.

Venus

Knock-Dead Gorgeous | Susan Teer is someone you don't find often, a Durham native. And even more important, she is one of our founding members of the local APS, way before the organization hooked up with the local pound to turn it into a shelter. She and husband Robb reside with a dog that is also a rare find, Chanel, the toy poodle.

One morning, as the shelter doors are opened, a noisy box is spotted. Inside is a quivering skeleton of a creature, flea-bitten and covered with mats as hard as brick growing right to her skin. The dog is placed in a puppy cage, not a run; at 2.5 pounds she is too small and would slip through the bars. Shortly after her discovery an anonymous call comes in, "Did you find a small dog in a box?" Yes. "That is my dog. She was stolen. I'll be in for her. My name is_____(lie)

Chanel Teer   12" x 12"   Oil on wood

and my phone number is_____(another lie)." The person never shows up, but because of the call, by law, the dog has to be held for a week, in the state that she is in!

She cries, she wails, she whimpers, the noises she emits never stop. The bathroom becomes the littlest dog's home. The crying is least disturbing there. She is inconsolable. Morale drops for all within earshot of the whimpering animal. She is pitied, but nobody wants to take her home. In walks Susan. "Susan, you must foster this dog!" Susan, a tall, immaculately groomed individual, is now on her way to the Cornwallis Road Animal Hospital, grimacing all the way.

The volunteer groomer starts at 9 a.m. with the 2.5 pound dog, working straight through to 3 p.m. Six hours later Susan gets a call to pick up the now-shaved and flea-less dog. Although the ex-pound resident still shows some fear, her mood is turning upwards. She understands she is being helped but is still too weak to show much appreciation. Susan and her daughter Kristin look over the bone-thin creature of French heritage and decide she needs the name that denotes the finest in elegance, Chanel. Little do they know that this starved ugly duckling of a pooch will indeed live up to her name.

Chanel

Susan introduces Chanel to everyone. "Wouldn't you like a poodle? She has cleaned up so well." The response is not positive. She is still thin and her self-confidence is paltry. She will not eat dog food, and her stomach has shrunk. The dog is truly near starvation. She is fed whatever the Teers are eating for dinner. Evidently this suits Chanel just fine, and she thrives.

Six months after arriving at the shelter, now settled into the Teer household, Chanel has doubled her weight, and her curly hair is a light-golden, peachie-bronze. People that now meet her ask, "Susan, is this one of your fosters? I want to adopt her." Ha! You had your chance! It is hard to believe this is the same dog that arrived anonymously in a box. As Susan unabashedly states, "She is simply knock-dead gorgeous!"

The toy poodle has an interesting effect on men, from plumbers, carpenters and yardmen to her human dad. They find their baby voice and coo, "Are you the prettiest girl in the world, or what?" Susan accepts and understands that this is simply a spell that Chanel seems to be able to cast over all men. At least once a week her husband asks, "Do you think she is the cutest dog in the world?" and "What did we do to get so lucky?" To make her world fully adjusted to her size, Robb has built a carpeted ramp up the stairs and placed stools strategically so she has access to all beds and couches.

What the dimunitive beauty loves most is Sterling the cat. Exactly double her size, the B&W long-haired domestic feline stays perfectly still when Chanel is in chase mode. She stares at the cat pleading, "Oh, please, let me chase you!" Occasionally the cat gives in and lopes along as the dog runs in hot pursuit. But more often they simply lounge in close proximity to each other.

Both animals love the Myrtle Beach house and even the car ride—four hours in Mom's lap. In fact, car rides are Chanel's thing. Saturdays, whether there is somewhere to go or not, she tells Robb it's time, and off they go for a ride around the block.

Temporary Placement | Susan DeLoatche is the other Susan at the Durham Animal Shelter. She has been volunteering in all capacities, except as veterinarian, for over twenty-five years. Also she has provided many with "temporary" homes, as witnessed by the motley crew that surrounds her now.

Angus, the most winsome of Scottish terriers, is picked up by Animal Control ten years ago. Jo, the assistant director, keeps the bone-thin, trembling black dog in her office. He is terrified of men wearing shoes, shakes continuously from any noise and winces at quick movements. Life has not been good. After a week

At Home with the DeLoatche Crew   20" x 32"   Oil on board

with Jo he is becoming calmer, and then after he joins the "foster home" of Susan D. he learns that life can be very good indeed.

Gracie

Entering the De-Loatche family room is a grinning white poodle with pink bows. I pick up my camera to catch the toothy grin, and off little Mitzi runs down the hallway barking. The poodle is found in the mean streets of Durham roaming with two Rottweilers. The owners are reported time and time again; finally the smallest of the threesome is picked up. Mitzi is a tough cookie, but still at the shelter she comes down with kennel cough. Susan brings her home temporarily to recuperate. A nice lady at the Forest of Duke is interested in adopting her. Mitzi understands this and snaps at her. Next another suitable home arrives for the sweet-looking dog; same deal, Mitzi comes with a smile—and a bite! Intentionally destroying both opportunities for a permanent home, she meanwhile showers Susan with love. Both Sue and husband Darrell "get it." She is home. Darrell takes her on adventures. Mitzi transfers approximately 90% of her love to him, bouncing and grinning all around him. On their pontoon boat out at the lakehouse, she is Queen of the Waterways.

Then there is Gracie, named after Gracie Allen, five pounds of adorableness. The Yorkie-toy-poodle-Maltese-mix was also picked up by our animal control officers. With her matted fur, blackened teeth, weakened

Mitzi of the Waterways   14" x 10"   Graphite on paper

condition, bad skin, it is estimated that she is easily fifteen years old. Susan takes her on. The dental procedure leaves her with four teeth, and her chin is permanently like cartilage, giving her a half-inch overbite. Then she is discovered to have pyrometra, a ruptured uterus. This is a life–threatening condition that can happen to unspayed dogs. Through diligent care Gracie makes a full recovery and is now thought to be only ten. Susan is delighted to have more time with her. As she explains, "Once you pick her up you can't put her down. She prances, runs, chirps like a little bird." And it is true, Susan has not put this dog down once since I got here.

The cat, Ms. Tubs, arrives directly after Susan's experience of watching indoor/outdoor Pepper become painfully emaciated from FELV. When obese, but healthy, indoor-only Ms.Tubs comes into the shelter, Susan brings her straight home. "A reprieve from my dear withering Pepper. I love both her size and personality. Oh yes, she is on a diet and is now only eighteen pounds." The Tubs appears to be fazed by nothing.

OK, so in this house of shelter animals how did English setter Benson, with papers, come to be? "My husband kept

Benson seeking squirrels

taking my dogs! I asked him to go get his own. He wouldn't. He wanted this one particular breed and they rarely come into the shelter." So, Darrell has continued to borrow his wife's companions for travel, walks and various adventures. Finally, Susan goes with her mother to Benson, North Carolina, to look at a litter of Darrell's desired breed. They choose the pup that seems least likely to take to hunting, an affectionate, gentle little guy. Being caged with other dogs would not suit sleek and docile Benson. Besides, he fits in here perfectly. Outside, I ask how to get his attention. "Mention squirrels." I do and he zips around to the house where he knows he will find some. Squirrels make him very excited.

Between Sue's mom and the two human kids, there are seven shelter rescues, ranging from dachshunds on up to a pair of Irish setters. Wait long enough at any shelter, with your name on the wish list, and just about every breed makes an appearance. Sure enough, a year after Benson's purchase, another English setter arrives at the Durham Shelter.

Detail with Angus, Mitzi & Benson

All in the Family

| Virginia and I met a couple of decades ago after I rolled into town in my VW camper just before her beloved Scotty died. Here she sits now at my studio/home with photos of the deceased Westy terrier. This painting is to celebrate a life well lived, an adoption success story.

Scotty

I started drawing animals by age three, and now others besides my parents are giving them wall space. I am impressed at how this woman who lives on the better side of the proverbial tracks sits easily in my place that looks and smells like fungi that popped up after a rain storm. In fact, after I move out, the place is bulldozed.

Many years later Virginia is at my open studio with her daughter Susan, whose animal family holds center stage on the gallery wall. Virginia is enthusiastic about my new place and is thrilled to recognize her grandpets in the large painting, but solemnly states that the paintings of Scotty and later Geoff, done so many years ago, are still her favorites. I'm wondering how to include them in *Dog Book,* when she says, "Shouldn't my Scotty be included? And, Susan, wouldn't your dad love to see his Toby in a book?" Susan agrees, we all agree.

Toby

Back at Virginia's I get to meet Toby, Ruby and Muffin who, like her daughter's companions, arrive as temporary borders. Foster animals always turn into permanent placement with these folks. Muffin they keep as she seems like an unlikely candidate for adoption, taking a long time to become

Muffin

completely housebroken. Her first year was spent in a dorm room, where she was fed but otherwise ignored. She is still a little aloof, but romps and plays full tilt with her two younger cohorts. She is twelve and, yes, is now housebroken.

All three are said to be shih tzus. Toby arrives as a small puppy and keeps growing and growing. When early on he discovers and uses the pet door on his own, Virginia's husband proclaims the puppy a genius and recognizes Toby as his very own! Virginia smiles, "Imagine, at age eighty my husband George got his first dog." Hadn't they been married fifty plus years and weren't there always several dogs in the household? Yes, but though he has lived with dogs for over fifty years, Toby touched a special cord.

Husband George has just received an honorary award, granted annually, from the Academy of Dermatology, The Dr. Clark Finnerud Award, when daughter Susan walks in with the third shih tzu, found in downtown Durham. "So, the name Rudy seemed appropriate, after the award, and so Rudy she became. She remained a foster for less than five minutes. She is a perfect dog. Susan and I drove to Florida with her and Gracie, and both behaved perfectly."

I mention how Sue finds her wonderful companions through

Geoff

Rudy

her volunteer work at the shelter. "Yes, even if she wasn't my daughter I would think a lot of her." Virginia shows me albums of photographs of her great grandpets, all foundlings. I realize there are many paintings and further chapters I could do about this family. The grandson has twin rescued Irish setters, the granddaughter lives with a menagerie, and it does appear that the families on both sides adopt all the animals they foster.

All in the Family   28" x 28"   Oil on board

Making the Time |

Working people who have huge jobs and find the time to volunteer inspire me. Phyllis Moore is a medical malpractice lawyer working most days 8 a.m. to 8 p.m., but every other weekend at the Durham Animal Shelter she is the Dog Team Volunteer leader. All bowls get washed, everyone is fed and walked, bedding is changed, food stocked, runs cleaned, dogs and puppies bathed, potential homes interviewed, dogs brought to visiting room; whatever else is needed is done. On weekends volunteers almost entirely run the shelter. There is much to do for a huge number of abandoned, lost, and surrendered animals.

At home Phyllis lives with three dogs and is currently fostering a terrier–mix puppy, Laine. One weekend this unweaned 1.5 pound pup is in the shelter washroom crying continuously. She needs to be fed five times a day. While the staff has tried to keep up with her feedings, there is little time to assure she is getting enough milk. Phyllis calms her down, deciding then and there she'll take on the role of mama dog. Thankfully she works only five minutes from home, and quickly the young one learns how to lap up milk from a bowl. Early on Phyllis notices something irregular, and as luck has it, all vets are closed. It means hastening off to the emergency animal hospital at 8:30 p.m. and waiting till 11:15 as a prolapsed rectum is corrected and sutured. Round worms, whip worms, and ever-deadly coccidia are the culprits. At the end of the minor operation, Laine's heart stops beating. CPR is administered and the puppy comes back from the tunnel of light. The girl I'm meeting today is a very bouncy, healthy, highly socialized, loving little creature, ready for adoption.

Midgie, an Eskimo spitz–Pomeranian, views Laine as a pint-sized pest. Phyllis found Midgie at Pet Depot as one of the featured animals at an adoptathon. For seven years she served as a training dog for vet technician students. Her rear flanks are shaved for bone–marrow aspirations, blood draws, and for whatever else is learned from a living learning tool. At the end of her seven years she is to be euthanized. A student sneaks her out the back door, and now here she is at the adoptathon. At her first real home, stairs are foreign to her and she is only used to relieving herself on cement. Everything scares her. She finds a closet where she feels safest. Seven years later, at age fifteen, she is still shy but is now happy and for her age, quite healthy.

During another weekend at the shelter, Phyllis is introduced to a corgi–Jack Russell–mix. He is scheduled for adoption, but when the family finds out he has tested positive for heartworm, they revoke their application. (A monthly pill is available to keep the deadly worms from forming in the first place.) As he is, the young dog can't be adopted. Phyllis takes him home as a foster along with the commitment to get him the treatment he needs to survive. The APS jumps on board and funds it. Charlie, the blind poodle–mix she adopted at age fourteen and has since died, is not at all bothered by young Opie, nor does he put out the truly ancient cocker–dachshund–mix Belle, also now deceased. Opie, one good–natured, all–around good guy, stays.

Dixie, the fourth dog I'm meeting here today, is the only one of Phyllis's adoptees that does not have a chronic disability or an illness to overcome. She is a petite, parti–colored cocker with a very decided prey–drive, chasing anything that dares move in the backyard. The bird feeder is her TV, holding her spellbound. Dixie was found through a website, *Annie's Rescued Friends—ARF, Inc.* (anniesrescue.org), named after a rescued cocker.

All breeds can be found through rescue groups, and all shelters and animal rescue organizations desperately need volunteers and foster homes. Without them they can't exist. As Phyllis can attest, special rewards await every volunteer. "I get back," she says, "much more than I give."

Laine, Opie, Midgie and Dixie   31" x 24"   Oil on board

A Safe Home | Southern Sister's Bookstore, the Durham Arts Council, and the Carolina Theatre are the three reasons to go downtown. Cookie Teer is the owner/operator of the feminist store offering a potpourri of crafts, cards, books, and always a dog working as receptionist. When Cookie decides to close the doors, many friends and supporters are sad, but she has solid reasons: Tickwood Bottom, twenty-five acres, a pond, and never less than four dogs.

Fanny

There is twelve-pound Fanny, who "will risk anything to be on a lap." She is a most unusual something wire-haired dachshund. A tornado had just touched down, the air is charged, and there trucking down Schley Road is a strawberry-blonde, wiry-haired dust mop with milk bottles swinging—she had recently given birth. The previous home can't be found. Fanny joins little Mini Bean, Pumpkin, and Rosey, and two years after that Sister joins them.

Mini Bean, a self absorbed, possibly Yorkie-poodle mix, gives flamboyant air kisses in her own manner of speaking. She does not know she isn't human. At only five pounds, of all the dogs she is the only one that retrieves. She could fetch all day. Rosey is another small wonder. The guess is she's a Lhasa apso-mix, and without a doubt a most remarkable bug-chaser. This canine

Sister

Rosey

Pumpkin

bug-catcher is remote, possibly has a touch of autism, and seems rather dotty, but when an insect flies or crawls in, swoosh! She pirouettes off the ground, spinning after her prey. As Cookie states, "When Rosey barks there is something to see, a bug, snake, turtle." She was chosen out of a litter the electrician had. She sucked on Cookie's earlobe, securing her a forever home.

The largest is Pumpkin, found in a kudzu patch as a golden ball of puppy fuzz. "He is my prince charming. He has a very male outlook." He herds the others and has a loud protective bark. At one time, with the rest of the gang, he slept on the queen-size bed. He is now banned due to his temperamental reaction to being disturbed. He hates being jostled in his sleep, and with four dogs and a human sharing the space this happens frequently. The human did not appreciate his growling, cursing loudly, and baring his teeth with each bump. So he now has his own pad at the foot of the bed.

Sister arrives at the bookstore hungry and thirsty, a sad-looking scraggly black dog with two apathetic teenage boys.

A Safe Home   30" x 30"   Oil on board

Cookie sees the chow-mix struggling. As she gives her water, she suggests to the teens, "Why don't you leave her here?" The animal drinks and drinks and drinks. One boy shrugs a shoulder in response, and they turn and leave. The black dog does not follow. Cookie phones the animal shelter. The dog warden arrives within the hour. Looking over the abandoned dog, she sums it up. "She won't get adopted. We have plenty of adorable puppies. She doesn't have a chance. She'll be euth-anized—it's your call." This is how the once near-death, now-stout, glossy-black Sister came to be the fifth dog out at Tickwood Bottom. "She is undemanding, unlike Fanny. She makes me feel safe. I can't imagine life without her." (Some dog catchers do more than catch dogs.)

When Cookie mentions she might put Tickwood Bottom on the market and downsize, folks are surprised. How do you leave paradise? Rolling hills, pond with gazebo, the majestic craftsman house with expansive porch, beautiful grassy lawns, and—Cookie elaborates—the mowing, the snakes, the ticks, more mowing, the hunters, dead ducks, and the skunk! The danger and inconvenience are ever-present, "like when I took all five dogs for their monthly appointment to the groomer's. Every month they all get the works, nails clipped, bathed, brushed, and fur trimmed according to season. Well, the next day, I mean not twelve hours later, my perfectly groomed dogs are hit by a skunk!" "Was the skunk ever found?" "Yes, by following the circling buzzards. I reported the incident to animal control. I was ordered to bring in the dead skunk to be tested for rabies. I explained that I had gotten rid of the body, far away. No way to retrieve or ever find it again. The government official was not happy with me. We all had to go in for rabies shots. This wasn't the final straw, but close to it."

There are twenty-five acres of invisible fencing, and the large dogs are well trained to respect it. Sister understands the concept of pain and learns the boundaries of the property quickly, not wanting to suffer. Pumpkin, having no experience with pain, doesn't get it. Cookie works tirelessly with him until he, too, realizes not to go outside the flagged area. For the

Mini Bean

larger dogs trained on the system, it works perfectly. It is an economical way to fence immense amounts of space. Pumpkin and Sister are safe within the confines of the prop-erty. There does not seem to be a need to train the smaller dogs, but one day the lodger that stays in the cabin crosses the road and Mini Bean follows. She is killed instantly by an oncoming truck. This is the final straw.

Cookie, Sister, Fanny, Rosie, and Pumpkin now live with-in city limits on a quiet side street; a pet door leads to the fenced half-acre yard. There are still plenty of bugs for Rosie to chase; Fanny just needs human attention, preferably all of the time; Sister might miss killing ducks; and certainly Pumpkin, the macho adventurer, misses the woods, the fields, the greater outdoors. With his human, however, he has taken to long walks and guarding the front walk.

Mushroom | Mushroom comes to live with us when I am thirteen. My sister Rachel is sixteen when she finds this pathetic stray in a parking lot. He is scared, filthy and very thin. We are cat people. Always, there is a family cat; a dog, Rachel realizes, will be a harder sell. "If this dog has to go, then I'm going too!" She is prepared to fight, but Dad takes the trembling terrier and gently gives him a bath. He shakes the whole time. Truly pitiful.

The dog cleans up well, and soon it's hard to remember when he wasn't with us, or should I say, with Rachel. The pair go to parties, concerts and drive-in picture shows. Rachel feels that when she isn't in school, where Mushroom isn't allowed, they should be together. Mushroom feels this even more strongly. He gets between her and any date, snarling out of the side of his mouth. The young men work hard to placate the mutt's unwavering glare.

At the dinner table Mushroom soon learns about gravity. At mealtime he becomes a canine vacuum. Soon, though, he discovers that my father, a picky eater, will secretly pass him all undesired food. Mom is sensitive to any criticism of her cooking. She expects all of us to be members of the clean–plate club. With Mushroom's help Dad is finally able to join the ranks. But on days that my father likes everything on his plate, Mushroom of course gets less, and so the whining begins. "Norman! Stop it!" Dad looks at Mom, all open-eyed, stupidly innocent. "What, Dear?" "You're feeding the dog again from the table!" "No, I'm not, honest." "Oh, yeah, then why is he sitting up begging and staring at you and whining?" My parents really aren't very used to dogs. Cats are so much

Mushroom   24" x 18"   Oil on board

Mushroom

more discreet at the table. They just sit on Dad's lap, stealthily accepting the scraps they prefer. Not Mushroom. He is fine with every morsel and ready to raise a protest if more doesn't quickly appear.

During the summer we go to the Lake House. Mushroom hates to get wet, so when we all go swimming he waits unhappily on the dock. On occasion when Rachel swims farther out or takes one of the boats, it becomes too much for him. He flings himself into the water and frantically heads out to his beloved person. When he reaches the boat, he is pulled on board. With the canoe this procedure can be very dicey. When we land on Round Lake Island with a picnic, Mushroom's begging practices are just as intense as they are at home.

Mushroom is limping again. Rachel turns around to study the lame dog. He continues his lopsided gait. Most pitiful. He stops stock still, his gaze on Rachel. Once he is assured that his terrible condition is noted, he continues on, only he has switched legs! Rachel acts like the dog is really hurt, telling him all kinds of sweet nothings and giving him a complete rubdown. The attention energizes him and he runs around in circles, the limp completely forgotten. Being cat people, we do not know how manipulative dogs can be.

When Rachel goes to college, so does Mushroom. Looking out the tall classroom windows onto the campus, Rachel sees him strolling about, achieving a pat here, a scratch there, or hanging out with other dogs and becoming generally known around campus. Class is over and he meets

R at the door. Wherever they go, Mushroom receives a hearty greeting while Rachel might have to settle for the casual hello.

After graduation Mushroom and Rachel move into the city. My sister's life is getting hectic, and the terrier is spending too much time alone. With my folks, especially since Mom is working only part-time, he will never be alone for long, so it is decided he should make the transition to Roanoke, Virginia. Here he lives with Siberian husky Kahotec, inherited from Rachel's friend Rob. All is fine until the husky gets a great big handsome German shepherd boyfriend, who views Mushroom as an interference. The shepherd camps out at our house. Mushroom has to be sneaked out the back to relieve himself. One day the big dog nabs him. My mother throws herself over the screaming twenty-five-pound terrier-mix. Somehow she gets the severely injured dog to safety and to the vet. Mushroom undergoes microsurgery to save his leg. He has pins installed that will never be removed, but remarkably he isn't left with a for-real limp.

My parents, as others apparently have done also, sue the people of the German shepherd for some very high vet bills. I wonder, if Mushroom had been neutered long ago when he first went to a vet, would he have been attacked? Possibly not. Hmm—the marking of territory, the years of whining as he tries to escape to get to every dog in heat for miles around. Did none of Mushroom's doctors try to educate my parents? They claim not. It is amazing that he lived seventeen years.

The painting of Mushroom now hangs in Madeline's room. My niece knows his stories well: how her mother found him, his fake limp, Grandpa feeding him under the table, his popularity on campus, how Mom and Dad had to spell out "car" whenever they didn't want him to beat them to it, his devotion to her mom.... Now till the end of time, Mushroom will be her guardian.

Love Story | It is months since my friend Wendy's border collie-mix, Destiny, has departed. Seven or so months later: "Don't tell me of other dogs, I'm not ready, I'll tell you when I'm ready." Somehow I doubt this. I check on her every day via phone, but she only talks of Destiny and cries or doesn't talk of Destiny and cries. I've talked many of my clients who have suffered loss into visiting the shelter or to being a foster home. Wendy is adamant about not heeding my advice. I pray and hope that over time there will be healing. At present it is not in sight.

I am enroute to a mural job when a B&W blur of a dog chases my car barking. I stop. When I get out of my truck, an oversized Lhasa apso leaps up on me repeatedly. This hyper mess of a dog is going to get hit out here, particularly with his uncontrollable behavior. I ask him, "Where is your home? Take me there." He does. The main feature of the drab, grey mill house is a clothesline from one end to the other draped with men's work clothes. The chain-link gate is pushed wide open. The woman that answers the door mumbles, "Oh, you found the damn loosu oopsu brother found," and then hollers back into the house, "Mah! Someone's here with Brat!" An elderly woman in bed in the living room asks if I want "it." "He's got papers, very valuable, could drive you crazy. My son got him at work. Thought he'd be good company. I don't want him. He's pretty, though." I agree to take him with papers and cage, but then they decide between themselves that the brother/son would be hurt and

angered. Best make it look like the dog ran away as they hoped he would.

I'm feeling most uneasy as I head to my mural job with purebred, paperless dog leaping about the cab, barking at every non-thing. I tie him to my scaffolding, get water for him

Jazz and Zoey's   21" x 18"   Oil on board

and my brushes, and then attempt to go to work. The dog barks continuously. Children stop and play with him. He jumps all over them, nibbling in his over-zealous fashion. As the parents snatch away their kids, I tell them the dog is available. They scurry off. I am getting no work done. An opera troupe troops out to see who is barking and making their practice impossible. A nice lady, a soprano, offers to take the enchanting-looking dog home to her fenced yard, adding that it's temporary only. I am deliriously grateful for the reprieve.

Back home I call Wendy to cheer her up. I tell her of the wildly obnoxious Lhasa apso…. "The singer's not keeping him?" I reply, "Of course not." To my shock, Wendy asks, "What's her number?" I attempt to discourage her. "No, you don't want this enfant terrible! There are many great dogs. No! I'll be hearing about his terrible behavior for years. No! You don't want this dog! Please!" Wendy asks again for the number of the bad dog's foster home. I give her the number, protesting the whole time.

Zoey

Less than an hour later Wendy calls, her voice all smiles. "I have a Lhasa apso!" I ask her why this hyperactive, unruly, loud beast? Why did she ignore all the good dogs I'd told her about? She says something about a childhood memory. Whatever, I brace myself to hear about new bad memories to be made. Yup, and sure enough every day a shoe is destroyed, a lunch is stolen, a plant is eaten, and, oh yes, he bites! I say it's not too late to find him another home. She won't hear of it. His horrible antics somehow charm her. Jazz has found the perfect home. I stop over. I am his savior and as such he must jump all over me. Wiggle, wiggle, all over the floor, and pee, too. I think he needs a mellower canine companion. Evidently, so does he.

Jazz is with Wendy only six months when an electrician leaves the front door insecurely closed. With a nudge of the door, Jazz is gone. The electrician takes off on foot in one direction while Wendy goes the other way by car, slowly, screaming his name. As she re-enters her block, she sees the escapee headed home. With him is a dog close to his size, but larger because of large wads of matted fur. The solid black dog is dragging a cable about twelve feet long. Jazz is very happy with his find. He is smiling, wiggling, nuzzling his new friend.

Wendy goes next door to dog-groomer Rema, who cuts off massive clumps of useless black fur. Had she not been found in the snow that arrived that night, she would certainly have frozen to death. Jazz has undoubtedly saved her life. His mom would do the rest with the help of others. Fully shaved, a cocker spaniel emerges and for now is dubbed Zoey.

At the vet it is discovered that the good-natured dog has

Jazz

a severe case of heartworm, was recently pregnant, and is now too weak to be spayed. Due to Jazz's hyper nature, she certainly can't stay with him and recuperate. A foster home without other dogs is found for the two months she will need to heal. A permanent home has not been lined up, as it is not known if she will survive. When the two months are up, she temporarily comes to Wendy's. Jazz is beside himself, hugging, kissing, dancing, prancing. His princess is home. That night the two curl up together on Wendy's (their) bed. Nah, she ain't goin' nowhere. Jazz's happiness is infectious, and Zoey's sweet nature does good things for the household. The cocker defers to Jazz and follows her new mom everywhere.

Over the next months I hear how the two are truly a couple, but they get along with other dogs, too. Wendy discovers a lonely Rottie named Slater, who spends sixteen-hour days alone in a fenced yard while his person is completing his residency at Duke University. Wendy offers to let him join them during the day. Next a neighbor down the street asks if whippet–Lab-mix Zena can join the pack. Why not? Then down the street two dogs are discovered tied up. Wendy talks their people into building a fence. They do, but during the day, guess what? Blackie and Tiger join the gang. At the moment a cuddly shepherd–chow–mix named Brownie is also being fostered at Jazz and Zoey's. They don't mind. They are delighted with all their new playmates that come along.

Detail from Jazz & Zoey's, the daily visitors

A Good Dog | Al Carson tells me I'll know his cubicle by the photographs of Sally, the canine joy of his life. I'm to pick up extra copies of an article he wrote on my current mural project. I easily find his space, the only one without photos of spouses, children and grandchildren. Al's booth is dedicated to Sally. He hands me a pile of tear sheets and an article he wrote on the Lab-shepherd-mix even though I am still years away from writing this book. When Al does a story on *Cat Book*, he asks, "And *Dog Book* is next? I have a great subject for your next project. My Sally is available." Obviously Sally has made the cut.

The year Al meets Sally he plans on two things, a trip to Las Vegas and a canine companion. The summer of 1994 is the worst. It is 105 degrees here and 125 degrees in Vegas. The trip is forgotten, the dog isn't. Driving along, Al hears the Triangle Trader on WPTF announcing that a litter of puppies is available. Sounds fine. He memorizes the phone number, makes the call and drives over to Apex. This was not love at first sight. As he puts it, "When Sally met Al, there was no spark of recognition. She was more intent on peeing on the carpet than on begging me to adopt her." The household she came from didn't ask a single question, nor did Al know of any to ask. The last dog he had given his heart to was Blackie, who was killed by a truck thirty-eight years ago. He hasn't risked the pet commitment since.

Neither Al nor puppy has a clue. Al looks at the dog and says, "You can be a good dog and we will get along. If you are a bad dog I'll shoot you in the head, bury you in the backyard, and no one will know. As it turns out, she is a good dog." Watching the home videos, The Sally Chronicles, I see the good puppy mangling Al's work boots, digging trenches in the

Sally   15" x 15"   Oil on board

garden bed, knocking someone down, and in general running amok. I am curious. "Tell me, Al, we are watching good behavior? Did you do any training?" "Yes, in puppy class, to get her to lie down I had to tackle her. She didn't go in for formal schooling, and there is no need for it." "Oh." Evidently, all she has to be is housebroken and not bite people hard. She has eaten an antique dining room set, an end table, and all the chairs along with other delectable items. When there was little to save, Al discovered crating, but then, "At age two the chewing magically stopped. She was no longer crated. I was going to be strict about her diet, only dry food. Two weeks after she arrived, while out camping with my buddies, I tell them not to feed her. Nobody listens. She is fed everything. Strict diet is over at eight weeks of age. But we did find out she doesn't like beer."

After Al and Sally settle into a perfect life, co-worker Flo Johnson tells him she's got the perfect woman for him. Her good friend Elizabeth Sevrence has a daughter who, like Al, is also a writer and, more importantly, is single. Liz and Flo brainstorm and decide that the two writers, both excellent cooks, should create a feast for them. The plan is just wacky enough so that Al and Liz's daughter Betsy go along with it. Al brings Sally, of course.

As happened with Sally, the chemistry is not instantaneous, but 600 emails later there is no denying a connection has occurred between the writers. The first time Al picks Betsy up he nonchalantly suggests she would be more comfortable in the back seat, as Sally is used to sitting next to him. Betsy thinks of bolting. "I know I should have run then! But then I knew I was hooked when I watched two hours of *The Sally Chronicles*. She sat between us on the couch and we held hands over her. Did I mention the fur? The first time I came over, Al tells me he has been cleaning all day. There is fur an inch deep everywhere. Cleaning was not going to take just one day."

A year passes and the two get married. When Betsy's daughters visit, together with grandchildren, the little ranch house overflows. They triple the floor plan by adding a second floor, playroom, and library/den with a screened-in porch. Sally is relegated to the great outdoors, dubbed Sallywood. The place is on a cul-de-sac with woods, no fencing. Sally is content outside being the greeter and meeter, and she has her play dates with dog friends on the block.

I stop by Al's *Herald Sun* cubicle. There are still images of Sally, but now photographs of a child with

deep dimples and corkscrew curls, along with other young people, grace the walls. At age fifty, Al skips raising human kids, but loves being a grandfather. Sally turns out to be great with young children, but then would you expect any less from a dog that never needed training?

Sallywood   12" x 9"   Graphite on paper

Living Large | China-dog and I are across from the mechanic's. The truck is getting its annual inspection. We are walking along the edge of the rolling grassy hill of Erwin Square when a black dog joins us. He and China exchange greetings; he jauntily walks alongside her. He has a wide grin and wagging tail. I put out my hand, he lunges back. Wow, that's weird! I try again. He backs away. Smiles with his eyes but physically says, "I'm scared, please respect that." Extreme shyness with humans, totally gregarious with fellow dogs? What makes his behavior more mysterious is that he can't be a feral dog or even come from a neglectful home. His coat is shiny and thick, and he borders on the portly. So where is his collar, his ID tags, and why is he hanging out by this busy road?

The mechanics say he seems to live in the field of Erwin Square. Punctually at 6:45 a.m. they see him coming through a cluster of trees, crossing into the field, sometimes romping with other dogs. I am really curious. What kind of people feed a dog this well, don't touch him, and just let him go? I am to do a community mural in this neighborhood, so I email my contact there about this dog. I hear from several people. The dog is famous.

Heather has noticed him six months back when she is out with Tyco, a shepherd-mix. They play so well that she lets Tyco off his lead. She can't get close to the black dog. She dubs him Ed, short for Erwin Square Dog. Ed's a little thinner than he is now, but he doesn't look terrible as some strays do. Intrigued by his personality, she decides to help him. Each day without fail she brings him breakfast in the field around 8 a.m. If she is late he shows up at her house two blocks away. Ed is punctual - he wants breakfast at 8 a.m. sharp. Heather ends her email requesting I don't contact animal control. If he is brought in, he will be deemed unplaceable and then destroyed.

Kaya also writes that she has been helping Heather with Ed. They want to socialize him and get him to a good, safe home. Kaya reiterates much of what Heather has said. Kaya feeds him dinner. She meets him at 5 p.m. sharp in the field. Kaya does not cook, so she buys a cookbook to figure out what Ed will eat. She explains that he must eat what she brings, as it is dosed with his vitamins and flea and tick medication. The competition is tough: from George's Garage daily scraps, from Parasade's Restaurant whole steaks, from untold others everything from leftovers to canned food. Kaya sees it as her responsibility to bring the meal that tops all others. His favorite is meatloaf with garlic and cheese. The 5 p.m. meal is delivered warm. At this point, capturing him seems remote. He is not motivated by food or attention. He has plenty of both.

Dee checks on Ed during the day. She works in a building by the field and has had her office switched so she can keep an eye on him. When it rains she places a tarp under a bush so he is not on wet ground and has some shelter. Before leaving she brings him last snacks. He greets her with wagging tail from his usual safe distance. A fourth person, Diane, affirms that the dog has a complex schedule. She has seen him near Northgate Mall south of town with other dogs. "He wakes at 6:45 a.m., comes out from under a fence by the stream, stretching and yawning. I call him Ferrie. I love this dog. He is the darling of the neighborhood. He's got a domes-

Detail from Ed of Erwin Square

Ed from Erwin Square   16" x 20"   Oil on board

tic routine, but it's just not in captivity. He owns himself, he is living large." She wishes he could stay free forever. She notices he is terrified as some boys go by on bikes. When questioned they tell her, "The damn bastard knocked up my dog!" Plans to catch Ed mount, for his own safety. Shortly after this incident I get an email about a litter of miniature Eds.

To Heather's shock and horror she sees the dog catcher's truck parked by the field. They have been notified. By law they must respond. Heather is told she has two weeks to get the dog off the field, off the streets. What to do? Through a local rescue group she borrows a trap; from a vet she gets drugs to sedate him. He gets a little drowsy, but not enough to enter the trap or let Heather approach. He vomits. This isn't working. His would-be captors send out notices: "PLEASE DO NOT

FEED ED!!! If he is not hungry he will not be enticed by the food in the trap. He has been discovered by animal control. We need to get him to safety." He has so many pit stops that even his beloved cheese meatloaf doesn't lure him into the crate. Kaya takes his favorite playmate, Henry, a pointer-mix, to the field. He won't follow them home. Heather tries the same ploy with Tyco. No deal.

Kaya brings a racket to play with, but Ed steals it, dancing about as she chases him. He laughs, he bumps her in the rear. Kaya spins around, Ed bounces back laughing. Sirens go off; Ed no longer howls in alarm. The other dogs have taught him the noise is nothing to be alarmed by. He is a good, happy dog, just not domesticated according to our terms.

Kaya's law-school exams are coming up. She can't study, she can't think of anything but that dog in the field. She urges her professors to postpone final exams until Ed is caught. Kaya has worked hard and long to find and follow her path; she is almost fifty, but nothing comes before getting Ed to safety. She packs food, a leash, collar, and trap. Pet care has been arranged for her four canine companions. She is not returning without Ed. In the field he sits beside her, five feet away. He likes her company. "Please, you must come with me." He smiles. They walk around the field while she explains the full ramifications: the better life he will lead, how much she loves him. He listens. She continues. It begins to rain. Five hours have passed. Ed never leaves her side. The rain is getting harder, she gives him another meal. He shows her some of his preferred bushes and trees that offer some protection. She pleads with him to follow her home. He seems to be listening. The rain is picking up force and it is cold. Eight hours have gone by. Kaya wonders if this will ever end. She spends the next two hours pleading with her fellow wet being. It is now pouring; she is wet, freezing and crying. She can't stop crying.

This feels like the longest day of her life. She has to go home, she is no good dead. Ed, evidently less affected by the inclement weather, stays by her. He is curious. She leaves at 10 p.m., fourteen hours after she has arrived, but Ed stays in the field. At home she collapses on her bed brokenhearted. All for naught.

5 a.m. she is up and feeds her crew. Getting all packed to stand watch in the field, she senses a presence. She can just make out a form in her front yard. It is Ed. He has never been here before. She runs inside and gets his buddy Henry. They play, eat breakfast, and then take a walk around the block. Back home she takes a ball and tosses it about. She is running out of ideas to keep Ed around when Monty starts barking from within the house. Kaya brings Monty out into the fenced yard. Ed enthusiastically runs along the fence with him. Kaya throws open the gate. Ed runs in and Kaya closes the gate.

I call Kaya, having received her elated email. "How is he?" "Asleep on the couch." After her exams are over I'll be meeting Ed for the second time, her for the first. As I drive down their street, I see out on a lawn three puppy toddlers at play. I park, of course. Their guardian tells me she is fostering them for the dog lady up the street named Kaya. Ed, I am told, adores the puppies.

Kaya is Asian, and I must mention that she and Ed have the same hair. Three dogs are sequestered in the back. Ed and Henry are here in the front room. Ed stands in the doorway with his odd little pointed ears, eyes squinting. Henry, a bulky pointer-mix, is on my lap washing my face. Ed has already been to the vet. He won't go in or near cars, so with his buddy Henry and Kaya they walk to Saint Francis Animal Hospital. The vet discovers Ed to be generally in fine health. However, he does have an eye problem; his bottom eyelashes, growing inward, are causing constant irritation. Kaya washes out his eyes several times a day and has begun to save for the operation he needs. A dog ophthalmologist in Cary comes highly recommended. Everyone that knows Ed looks forward to seeing how he will further blossom when he is no longer impeded by pain and blurred vision.

Three other dogs, all large, emerge from the back room. Now there are three large dogs vying for my lap. Kaya holds pretty Lola, as it is not unusual for her to bite. I ask Kaya if she came from an extreme animal background. "*Au contraire*! My mother is Japanese and she raised me. We don't have pets. Some have, but it's just not common practice. I went to get a dog six years ago when I was told they make good running partners. I saw a dog as an accessory. The shelter read me perfectly and would not let me adopt the malamute hybrid I wanted. But I am Japanese, I am stubborn. I wore them down and adopted King, the most difficult dog I could have adopted." Being ultra-alpha, King provided a crash course for Kaya, and she discovered something special she had not known about herself—an extraordinary talent in handling canines along with a great compassion and respect for them. How strange to live forty-four years without even a goldfish, now to be known as the "dog lady down the street."

Ed in the Hood   12" x 9"   Graphite on paper

A Girl and Her Dog | I'm walking with my neighbor Kathy and China-dog when we cross the road into the next neighborhood. As we go by a house with a picket fence, a gangly burgundy-brown youngster of a hound peers over at us. Large soulful eyes beckon China; the young dog's snout rests atop a post. She almost audibly says, "Come play with me." China responds by trying to leap into the yard, nearly breaking my arm. "OK! I get the point!" So now at the front door the three of us stand as a young woman answers the door. "Yes?" "Your puppy has asked my dog to come play in her yard." With a quizzical expression, Jennifer directs us through her house to the backyard.

China and the chocolate Lab-English pointer-mix, Belle, greet each other with a simultaneous leap. China has at least twenty-five pounds on her new friend so she enjoys knocking her over and pinning her to the ground. Belle, although a little alarmed by her new and aggressive buddy, discovers she can outrun the somewhat older dog. Belle is fast. She springs off the deck, landing ten feet out, bolting over stocky China's head. Belle's young human, Annie, yells, "China, don't hurt Belle." The young dog is seven months old, a tall, lean fifty pounds, and just puppy enough to let out some terrifying yelps, to let all know China has gone too far. Amazingly, she comes back for more. When we leave, Jenn asks when we will come back. That was half a year ago and since then these dogs get to exhaust each other one to three times a week, happily so.

I was surprised that these seemingly intelligent people would have such a large springy dog with their child just turning five. "Well, this was not in the plan," Jenn explains. "We told Annie, when you're older, when you can help with a dog." But there was no way to stop or foresee this curve ball that would become a homerun.

Sam is a friend and peer of Annie. Sam's grandparents live in Holly

China

Springs on a farm. The unaltered farm dogs mated, producing a large litter of brown mix-breed puppies. On a playdate Annie visits the farm with Sam; the puppies are only a couple of weeks old, bundles of soft warm fur making little baby grunts and smelling of doggy milk. Annie is mesmerized. When Jennifer picks her

Detail of Annie & Belle

daughter up, she reiterates the "when you're older" mantra, but Annie can't hear it. She is on a mission: "Mom, let's call Dad."

Jennifer phones Dave on her cell phone and hands it to Annie, who asks to speak with her father. Jenn hears this half of the conversation: "We went to Sam's place. We played with Betty (a horse), we got to feed cows, and, Dad, they've got puppies (punch line)! Dad, let's bring one home. It will be all right, I promise." Jennifer knew then that a puppy was coming home now, not in a couple of years. Oh, what the heck, the child's first words, after all, were "ruff, ruff", not "mama," but her husband was raised in the country. Animals did not come in the house. Dave was going to have a lot to get used to.

During the wait for the puppies to be weaned, Jennifer buys a book on breeds and another on raising and training a puppy. Neither Dave nor she being dog people, they both read the book thoroughly. Jenn finds a good vet and has many questions answered. Their half-acre yard is already fenced. At Petsmart they go down the checklist, buying indoor and outdoor water bowls, ceramic food dishes, chew toys, pull toys, balls with handles, large crate, large bed, collar, ID tag, leash, bones, puppy chow and bone-shaped mat. The total is a little over $300. Dave is sighing loudly and rolling his eyes. He can't believe how he has been conned. This is insanity.

Enter the puppy! The first couple of weeks Annie's mom protects the small dog from inexperienced hands. The next couple of months Jennifer protects her daughter from the growing pup's sharp teeth and claws. What to call her? Annie suggests Cinderella. Her mom asks how she thinks it would sound hollered off the back porch? "Ooh, no, I don't want to be an evil stepsister. How about Belle?" Belle she is!

Belle and Annie's parents are out to dinner with business associates. They talk of how they are not animal enthusiasts, but have managed to produce an extreme one in their daughter. Dave mentions the cost of becoming such an enthusiast. The business associate laughs. "That's nothing! Our dog cost $1,200 before I bought his house, bowls, toys, vet visits." Jennifer looks across at her smiling husband. He now knows he got off cheap: only $300 for equipment, and the dog was free, free, free! He got a true bargain. This country boy likes that.

Belle and China are now nearly the same weight, with Belle standing four inches taller at the shoulders. They knock each other down in unison, then China stands still as Belle leaps around antelope style, and in fact some days Belle plays very aggressively. At those times, Annie might shout, "Belle, don't hurt China!"

Annie and Belle   34" x 28"   Oil on board

The Missing Puzzle Piece | On the streets of New York a vendor sells bobbing-headed turtles made out of nut shells. I buy two, thinking of Cindy Vega's new pets, red-ear slider turtles. Back in Durham I stop by the blacksmithing shop, Vega Metals/Cricket Forge. The showroom is full—looks like they're packing for a show. A small puppy bounces up to me. "Hey, who is this?" From around the corner Cindy responds, "Annabelle!"

"I thought Francis said no more animals?" "She fits, she's the missing puzzle piece." That's believable. For years George, a basset-beagle, was Vega Metals' official greeter. When he died it just didn't feel right to even try to replace him, but then, at the homestead, there are a dozen birds, cats sequestered in different areas, Cindy's mother-in-law's chow-mix companion, Valentino, turtles, and enough plants to give the look of a small rain forest to the 3,000-plus square feet.

Back at their place I see Annabelle loves her home. She runs around like a little locomotive, making a continuous low growl. She zooms around the couches, around the dining room table, around the floating stairs, encircles part of the rain forest, lands at our feet, out of breath and ready to nibble on my fingers.

Cindy goes to Petsmart for bird/turtle/cat food. The adoption table is set up with three lively puppies. She naturally gravitates to the table, as she has a growing yearning for canine companionship. She finds herself filling out an adoption form and taking the contact information should her husband agree. She also wants to give herself more time to prepare, to think about things.

The husband says, sure. Actually, asking Francis is just a formality. Cindy drives the country roads out to Timberlake, where kennel owner Rebecca Hessee has rescued a litter of eight from under a neighbor's house. The neighbor had been feeding the mother, and that was it; all are covered with fleas and filth. Rebecca cleans them up and places half of them in well scrutinized homes by the time Cindy arrives. Now one lucky pup is about to enter a life of pampering in a helluva stately place. At the Timberlake garage, fixed up as a temporary nursery, Cindy gets a full head-on stare from the puppy that is to become Annabelle. Cindy has been chosen!

Rescuing and placing animals Rebecca does continuously. She describes her current boarders: "Six are paying clients, ten are freeloaders." The ten she hopes to place in good homes, but then she gets a call that will very possibly be bringing the freeloader count closer to thirty. The local shelter is euthanizing most of the dogs to make room for the thirty plus pitbulls confiscated in a dog-fighting bust. Rebecca and a friend are going to take all the dogs they possibly can and make a public plea for foster and permanent homes. Cindy leaves before she finds herself taking the rest of the litter.

At home it's late, the puppy has fallen asleep on their bed. Cindy goes to remove her, but Francis pleads, "Oh, let her stay." Cindy explains that if she stays this will be where Annabelle Sweetpea Vega sleeps for many, many years to come. Francis feels that waking her up and removing her would be cruel. Annabelle sleeps between her humans every night.

In the morning she is reluctant to get up; she loves having both her humans with her. At the shop she sleeps on top of the couch, with Cindy in full view at the computer or talking with clients. Francis intermittently comes through to take her for walks. Sometimes she is so relieved to see him she pees. "I don't know why. She sees him all day."

Back home at her palace, she finds a watch, glasses, scissors and repositions them. Socks she actively steals, enjoying Cindy's attempts to get them from her. At the dining room table she is giving Francis her big-eyed puppy look. I ask, "You feed her from the table?" Francis proudly replies, "Yes, I do. If it was up to me she'd have a place at the table." Cindy interjects, "At some point we have to draw the line and realize she is a dog." But why? She doesn't.

Annabelle Sweetpea Vega   18" x 18"   Oil on board

Chez Chien, or Skyler's House | Through the personals, China-dog and I meet the French artisan Philippe and German shepherd Skyler in order to go sailing on his boat. We drop anchor near a deserted island beach; humans swim, dogs wade. We enjoy a simple lunch of bread, cheese, cherries, and wine. Tanned and tired, we head to the mountain town of Swannanoa to tour Philippe's rock home, with its indoor and outdoor fire places, thick Persian rugs, handmade furniture and antiques, and oil paintings by artists he knows covering the walls. Skyler is showing China her backyard. It goes back 200 feet, or more. Her dog house is a log cabin six by eight, with two windows that open, family pictures on the wall, custom mattress, and a front porch. My head spins. China and I want to live here.

Looking out on the large lawn with its ancient grape arbor and its peach, cherry and apple trees, we eat a leisurely meal that Philippe has prepared in no time. He is a boat builder, fine carpenter, accomplished photographer, and a chef who cleans up after he cooks! As the sun sets, I ask, "Are we in love yet?" Philippe responds in the negative. This is not what I wanted to hear. After throwing my stuff in the ole truck with China loaded up, I yell as I spin off, "I like Skyler better than you! And unfortunately she is not in *Dog Book* and neither are you!"

A year passes while Philippe continues to send me funny and bizarre emails. Perhaps it's just an oversight with his address list, but whatever, I realize we are not enemies, so when I'm scheduled for a few events in his area I call. "Hi, it's me. I need to ask you three favors: help me hang a show, get all your friends and family to my book signing, and Skyler and you show us some great hiking." Once he figures out who "me" is, he answers in the affirmative and, not expected at all, he invites us to stay at his castle. All is not lost!

We arrive at Philippe's and Skyler's at 11 p.m. He is flying in from the Caribbean where he has been sailing. Did he miss his flight? Skyler greets us and happily lets us in the back door. Perhaps at age eight her guard-dog days are over or she recognizes us from a year ago. I set up camp in his den.

Skyler

Around 4 a.m. China is barking loudly. Philippe is home. "Hello, Me. How is *Dog Book* coming?"

Skyler is the last dog to make it into the book, a boat almost missed. The shepherd was found on a Savannah, Georgia, highway, all skin and bones, scrapes and sores, obviously one neglected and abused dog. This is the condition she arrived in at Michael Redfox's German shepherd rescue ranch, which primarily takes in retired police and search and rescue dogs. Philippe has envisioned adopting an older canine hero to share the "good life." Also, he loves the idea of a dog arriving already trained, a total ready-made housemate. Skyler does not have the illustrious past of a police or SAR dog, but she is in great need. Her ears are down, tail hidden under her body, and she glues herself to the floor in terror when confronted with loud noises or quick motions. Once in her new home, she is very self-protective and bites. Philippe replaces many torn jeans. Six years later the Skyler I know is friendly and happy, ears up, face bright, tail wagging, and frolicking in the yard like a puppy. Now she only nibbles folks for attention, announcing, "Hey, I'm here." She wants to be a part of everything.

At Philippe's I have paints and brushes but no canvas. He runs around gathering a variety of surfaces to paint on: wood with worm holes, warped wood, nothing very promising. "What about that ugly landscape over your bed?" Without a word, Philippe gets it and dislodges the frame. His daughter bought the palette-knife eyesore at a yard sale years ago for the frame. She is amazed that her dad gives it wall space. We sand down the paint ridges and I use the old painting as an under-painting poking through. With a half-inch brush I paint Skyler's log cabin with grape vines and on the right-hand side a sitting Skyler. A three-hour masterpiece. Philippe asks what this over-painting will cost him? "A trip to France? The antique wood stove in your garage? Oh, what the hell, we'll just move in!"

Skyler with Her Log Cabin   24" x 36"   Oil on board

resources

LOW COST NEUTER/SPAY PROGRAMS

For low cost spay/neuter programs in your area please call:
SPAY/USA
1-800-248-SPAY

EDUCATION

The Culture and Animals Foundation is a nonprofit, cultural organization committed to fostering the growth of intellectual and artistic endeavors united by a positive concern for animals. They hold the Annual International Compassionate Living Festival the first weekend in October.

Culture and Animals Foundation

3509 Eden Croft Dr., Raleigh, NC 27612
919-782-3739, Fax:919-782-6464
www.cultureandanimals.org

A monthly magazine for caring dog owners put out by the veterinary school at Tufts University, with the latest on animal medical breakthroughs and behavior:

Your Dog, Subscription Services,
P.O.Box 420234, Palm Coast, FL 32142

This largest no-kill animal shelter in America offers information on how to set up a similar program in your area; also a great place to take a volunteer work vacation:

Best Friends Animal Sanctuary

5001 Angel Canyon Drive, Kanab, Utah 84741-5000
Tel: 435-644-2001

Seminar Videos presented by some of the leading authorities in the fields of dog behavior, training and health:

www.TawzerDogVideos.com

(208) 466-3033

Foster Home Network - www.petfoster.org

About the joys and needs of pet fostering, and tips for developing successful foster programs.

Critter Magazine - www.crittermagazine.com

Free monthly magazine supported by local business advertising and running ad pages at no cost to local shelters and rescue groups in order to showcase animals available for adoption. The publication also features educational articles, a Kids' Page, and a calendar of events. For information about publishing a Critter Magazine in your community, contact Elaine Lite at crittermag@mindspring.com, or call (828) 255-0516

Comprehensive source of information located in California:
Rescuers.com

A helpful, amusing, attractive quarterly with a heart for dogs and their people:

The Bark

2810 Eight Street, Berkeley, CA 94710
(877) 227-5639   www.thebark.com

A remarkable literacy program in Utah that should be everywhere:
R.E.A.D. (Reading Education Assistance Dogs)
www.therapyanimals.org

Adoption Books (recommended by writer Karen Derrico, New Sage Press, 1999)

Adopting a Great Dog by Nona Kilgore Baur
Choosing a Shelter Dog by Bob Christiansen
Save That Dog by Liz Palika
Shelter Dog by M.L. Papurt, DVM
Second Hand Dog by Carol Lea Benjamin
The Adoption Option by E. Rubenstein/S.Kalina
The Right Dog For You by Daniel Tortora

YOU DESIRE A CERTAIN BREED?

Specific breed rescue groups offer excellent places to look. One site that lists many such:

www.ecn.purdue.edu/~laird/animal_rescue/

If you do not have web access, list your name with your local shelter; in all probability your breed of choice will show up.

A Rottweiller rescue group - www.ssrr.org and the cocker spaniel rescue group, www.anniesrescue.org, are mentioned here in *Dog Book*, but there are hundreds more.

PRODUCTS

Before you or anyone you know gives up on an animal, please try the remedy Abandonement & Abuse. Flower essences expedite the recovery of animals acting out due to fear or trauma of any kind, discharging negativity in a benign way. Here are some of the remedies offered for the health and emotional wellbeing of animals: Anxiety, Digestive Woes, Flea Free, Jealousy, Outbursts, Separation.

Green Hope Farm
P.O. Box 125
Meridan, NH 03770
Tel: 603-469-3662

Health food for animals:

Wysong: "The Thinking Person's Pet Food"
Wysong Corporation
1880 N. Eastman Road
Midland, MI 48642
www.wysong.net

Raw, organic, balanced diet for optimum health in animals:

Nu Dimensions Nutrition, Inc.
(919) 848-4071
www.nudimensionsnutrition.com

Safe Traps from a company that does not manufacture the crippling leghold trap:

Tomahawk Live Trap
P.O. Box 323
Tomahawk, WI 54487
Tel: 800-272-8727

An organization which has "Expedition Quality Gear for the Everyday Dog," leads hikes, does photograph-ID registration with a toll free relocation number, has a "doggie cafe," throws benefits for various animal advocacies, and publishes "Dog Outreach Program":

Trail Hound Gear Shop, Asheville, NC
TrailHounds.com
(866) DOG-PACK (364-7225)

For miniature and toy sized dogs:

Unique Accessories, Inc
1625 Larimer Street, Suite 1206, Denver, CO 80202
www.uniaccs.com
1-800-831-8929

William Secord Gallery, Inc.
When in New York City visit the only gallery to specialize in 19th century dog paintings. In the meantime get acquainted on-line at dogpainting.com. Mr. Secord has authored three volumes of massive magnificent art books:

A BREED APART, *The Art Collections of The American Kennel Club and The American Kennel Club Museum of The Dog*

DOG PAINTING, *The European Breeds*

DOG PAINTING, 1840-1940, *A Social History of the Dog in Art*

William Secord Gallery, Inc.
52 East 76th Street, New York, NY 10021
(212) 249-0075

ALTERNATIVE ANIMAL CARE

Working exclusively through phone consultations, my homeopathic vet offers both less invasive treatments and support for more mainstream methods:

Charles Loops, CVM
38 Waddell Hollow Road
Pittsboro, NC 27312
(919) 542-0442

Reiki practitioner, Anita works with the art-of-healing touch for animals both in person and via phone. "Healing Touch" is her story in *Cat Book* :

Anita Anglin
P.O.Box 1294
Pittsboro, NC 27312
(919) 545-2390

Healing touch for animals workshops:

Komitor Healing Method, Inc.
P.O.Box 262171
Highlands Ranch, CO 80163-2171
(303) 470-6572
www.healingtouchforanimals.com

Books recommended by Susan King, CMT
(Canine Massage Therapist, www.companionchi.com):

The Healing Touch, Dr. Michael W. Fox
The Encyclopedia of Natural Pet Care, C.J. Puotinen
The Well Connected Dog, Amy Snow and Nancy Zidonis
Four Paws, Five Directions, Cheryl Schwartz, DVM
The Last Chance Dog, Donna Kelleher, DVM
The Nature of Animal Healing, Martin Goldstein, DVM
Keep Your Dog Healthy the Natural Way, Pat Lazarus

Books recommended by Linda Tilley,
Dog Trainer Extraordinaire.

The Quilt-Free Dog Owner's Guide, Diana Delmar
Leader of the Pack, Baer & Duno
Why Does My Dog? John Fisher, DVM
On Talking Terms With Dogs, Turid Rugaas
Help for Your Shy Dog, Deborah Wood
So Your Dog's Not Lassie, Fisher & Delizio
Pet Allergies: Remedies for an Epidemic, Plechner & Zucker
Raw Meaty Bones, Tom Lonsdale, DVM
What Vets Don't Tell you About Vaccines, C. O'Driscoll Bones
Would Rain From the Sky, Suzanne Clothier
Search & Rescue Dog Training Methods, Amer. Res. Dog Assoc.
HSUS' Pet First Aid by Bobbie Mammato, DVM, MPH
ASPCA's Complete Dog Care Manual, Bruce Fogle, DVM

MISCELLANEOUS

www.freeplay.org
Lists dog parks that have websites and gives information for starting a dog park.

www.Traveldog.com
A site with lots of helpful information. As a member, your canine companion can get up to 65% off on lodging. They have a complete listing of pet-friendly accommodations, great destinations, help with car sickness, etc.

Camp Gone to the Dogs
The ultimate dog vacation! Fun classes, seminars and plenty of canine socialization.

Camp Gone to the Dogs
P.O.Box 600
Putney, VT 05346
(802) 387-5673

Camp Winnaribbun

For the ultimate quilt-free vacation in a beautiful location:

Camp Winnaribbun
P.O. Box 50300
Reno, NV 89513
(775)348-8412

Books recommended by Emily Eve Weinstein

THE DOG THAT RESCUES CATS
A fascinating paperback written by Philip Gonzalez and Leonore Fleischer. (See pages 25-27 in this book.) www.TheGinnyFund.org

HELLO, GOODBYE, I LOVE YOU *The Story of Aloha, a Guide Dog for the Blind* by Pamela Bauer Mueller Based on a true story about 12-year-old Diego raising the guide dog, Aloha. Great gift for young readers.

THAT DOG WON'T HUNT
Ten true stories of pedigreed rescued dogs written and illus-trated by my friend Valerie Blettner. Beautiful little gift book. www.GrinningBeagle.com

CONVERSATIONS WITH ANIMALS
By Lydia Hiby with Bonnie S. Weintraub
Amazing stories of Lydia Hiby's conversations with animals.

THREE CATS, TWO DOGS: *One Journey Through Multiple Pet Loss* by David Congalton. Very moving helpful book.

WHEN YOUR PET OUTLIVES YOU:
Protecting Animal Companions After You Die
By David Congalton and Charlotte Alexander

UNFORGETTABLE MUTTS, *Pure of Heart Not of Breed*
Beautifully written stories by Karen Derrico, with comprehensive reference pages.

www.maydayformutts.org, originated by Ms. Derrico, easy access to becoming active on behalf of dogs.

China and Cleatus   5" x 10"   Graphite on paper

David Jessee

China and Emily

Emily Weinstein has had numerous solo shows in galleries and museums. She paints interior and exterior murals for both private and public venues, does commissioned portraiture, takes vacations to do landscape painting and go hiking with China-dog. She also lives with cats Sophia, Eva, Casey and Roma in the Research Triangle area of North Carolina. For more information, visit her website at WeinsteinArt.com.